Challenging Gender Norms

Five Genders among Bugis
in Indonesia

Challenging Gender Norms

Five Genders among Bugis
in Indonesia

SHARYN GRAHAM DAVIES
Auckland University of Technology

Case Studies in Cultural Anthropology: George Spindler
and Janice Stockard, Series Editors

Australia • Brazil • Canada • Mexico • Singapore
Spain • United Kingdom • United States

Challenging Gender Norms: Five Genders
among Bugis in Indonesia
Sharyn Graham Davies

Senior Acquisitions Editor: Lin Marshall
Assistant Editor: Leata Holloway
Editorial Assistant: Danielle Yumol
Technology Project Manager: Dee Dee Zobian
Marketing Manager: Caroline Concilla
Marketing Assistant: Teresa Jessen
Marketing Communications Manager: Linda Yip
Project Manager, Editorial Production:
   Christy Krueger
Creative Director: Rob Hugel
Art Director: Maria Epes

Print Buyer: Linda Hsu
Permissions Editor: Roberta Broyer
Production Service: Sara Dovre Wudali,
   Buuji, Inc.
Copy Editor: Kristina Rose McComas
Cover Designer: Carole Lawson
Cover Image: Sharyn Graham Davies
Cover Printer: Thomson West
Compositor: International Typesetting
   and Composition
Printer: Thomson West

The logo for the Cultural Anthropology series is
based on an ancient symbol representing
the family: man, woman, and children.

All photos are reprinted with the permission
of the author except where noted.

Cover Photo: Bissu contacting the spirit world.

Printed in the United States of America

2 3 4 5 6 7 10 09 08 07

Library of Congress Control Number:
2006929927

Student Edition: ISBN-13: 978-0-495-09280-3
   ISBN-10: 0-495-09280-0

Thomson Higher Education
10, Davis Drive
Belmont CA 94002-3098
USA

For more information about our products,
contact us at:
Thomson Learning Academic Resource
Center
1-800-423-0563

For permission to use material from this text
or product, submit a request online at
http://www.thomsonrights.com.
Any additional questions about permissions
can be submitted by e-mail to
thomsonrights@thomson.com.

For my friends in South Sulawesi who shared their lives with me and who added a richness to my life that words cannot express.

Tarima kasi maéga pattulutta'. Puangngallataala mpale'ki'.

Contents

Foreword

ABOUT THE SERIES

The Case Studies in Cultural Anthropology Series was founded in 1960 under the joint editorship of George and Louise Spindler, both anthropologists at Stanford University. Since that time, more than 200 case studies have been published, and the series has enjoyed wide readership in college and university classrooms around the country and abroad. New case studies are published every year. With Louise Spindler's death in 1997, the series was left with one editor until Janice Stockard became an editor in 2005. Janice is an accomplished author and editor and brings powerful expertise in marriage, gender, family, and technology, as well as extensive editorial experience.

The case studies were initially conceived as descriptive studies of culture intended for classroom use. By design, they were accessible, short, and engaging. Their authors were anthropologists who had conducted extensive field research in diverse societies, experienced professionals who had "been there." The goal was to introduce students to cultural differences, as well as to demonstrate the commonalities of human lives everywhere. In the early years of the series, each case study focused on a relatively bounded community—a cultural group, tribe, area—that could be distinguished by its own customs, beliefs, and values.

Today the case studies reflect a world transformed by globalization and an anthropology committed to documenting the effects of the vast cultural flows of people, information, goods, and technology, now in motion the world over. In this twenty-first century, the greater pace and reach of globalization have created an infinite number of meeting points for people and cultures—and multiplied the sites and contexts for cultural change. In 1960, it was our task to present examples of the diversity characterizing the world's cultures; today it is our task to describe and analyze the impact of globalization on the diverse cultures of the world. To this end, we have recently published an anthology, *Globalization and Change in Fifteen Cultures: Born in One World, Living in Another* (2007), that focuses on the processes and impact of change on cultures represented in the Case Studies in Cultural Anthropology series.

In this series, we have set out to accomplish several objectives. One is to describe the distinctive features of the cultures of the world. Another is to analyze the sweeping changes under way, resulting from the processes of globalization, migration, urbanization, and modernization. Thus for anthropologists today, the task is both to document the cultural transformations and to decipher the ways in which the particular forms that change takes are influenced by the distinctive features of specific cultures. A no less daunting task is to understand the meaning of these changes for the people who live with them.

Globalization and cultural change in the twenty-first century present anthropologists with the challenge of studying (and writing about) extraordinarily complex processes. We invite you to experience this complexity in the current products of our series, as well as in the new anthology.

ABOUT THE AUTHOR

SHARYN GRAHAM DAVIES was born in Tasmania, Australia, in 1974. After spending a year in Ohio, USA, as a Rotary exchange student, she returned to Tasmania keen to study French and political science. With neither of these courses being offered, Sharyn reluctantly enrolled in Indonesian and Asian Studies and, much to her surprise, fell in love with both. In 1997, Sharyn received a First-Class Honors Degree and the following year took up a PhD scholarship at the University of Western Australia, where she jointly enrolled in Anthropology and Asian Studies. Sharyn was supervised by Dr Lyn Parker and Dr Greg Acciaioli. During her PhD research, Sharyn spent over a year living in Indonesia, and she continues to return to the archipelago frequently. In 2003, Sharyn took up a tenured lectureship position at Auckland University of Technology, where she was employed to develop the Anthropology program within the School of Social Sciences. Outside academia, Sharyn enjoys traveling, hiking, and karate, where she has earned a 1st Kyu brown belt in Goju Ryu. In November 2005, Sharyn married her karate instructor and the love of her life, Thomas Graham Davies.

ABOUT THIS CASE STUDY

In this case study, an anthropologist explores the rich gender diversity among Bugis, the largest ethnic group in South Sulawesi, Indonesia. Sharyn Graham Davies' lively ethnographic account takes readers on a journey beyond dichotomous constructions of gender to explore the multiple genders of Bugis society. In all, she documents five genders, each recognized, named, and occupying a distinct status.

As context for her analysis, the author situates each gender within both historical and contemporary Bugis society, comparing and contrasting third, fourth, and fifth genders alongside and against the local cultural meanings of "woman" and "man." For each of the five genders—including transgendering females (calalai), transgendering males (calabai), and androgynous shamans (bissu)—Davies identifies several dimensions that together constitute their distinct subjectivities. Thus, this case study explores the lifestyles, behaviors and clothing, social and ritual roles, sexual practices, and erotic desires of five different genders. For her ethnographic portraits, the author draws on formal interviews and informal conversations with persons of each gender, as well as on firsthand observations and experiences participating in everyday routines and social events, such as weddings, festivals, and spirit possessions. Today, Bugis live in an Islamic society and a nation–state (Indonesia) where powerful religious and political discourses about ideal family structure and hierarchy and proper gender behavior and sexuality would appear to threaten their cultural world. Davies examines Bugis responses to these challenges, including resistance, accommodation, and co-existence.

In her ethnographic exploration of the multiple genders specific to Bugis, the author introduces fundamental issues and key concepts in gender theory. These she frames as opening questions and later recaps in concluding discussions to each chapter. Among the issues she considers is, "What is this thing called gender?" This question becomes both the organizing theme of Chapter Two and its title. Other topics in gender theory that are introduced for consideration and discussion are the relationships of gender to biological sex and bodies, gender identity to sexuality, and gender to marriage.

In addition to the inherent appeal of the topic of multiple genders, this case study offers an adventure in fine ethnographic writing. The author's writing style is at once graceful, analytical, and engagingly reflective. With regard to this last quality, Davies' writing seems almost to transport her audience into the differently gendered world of Bugis society. That world comes alive through her descriptions of personal encounters with friends, "family," and field informants—and through her accounts of their reactions to her, a cultural outsider with a different gender subjectivity. This case study also opens a door into the repertoire of ethnographic methods used by anthropologists and as such provides readers with an introduction to fieldwork practice. The author's field notes and journal entries are skillfully woven around accounts provided by persons representing each of the different gender subjectivities. In response to the author's presence and questions, these cultural informants describe their social worlds and relate their personal stories, including their decisions to self-identify and live as transgendering females or males. In the case of the androgynous shamans (bissu), we learn about the distinctive signs and behaviors that signify this fifth gendered identity. In *Challenging Gender Norms: Five Genders among Bugis in Indonesia,* readers will enjoy taking part in Sharyn Graham Davies' first observations, initial assumptions, field mishaps, new questions, fresh insights, and ultimate understandings of a differently gendered people and world.

Preface

This ethnography explores a society that recognizes not just two gender categories, like most societies, but rather more. The setting for the ethnography is the Indonesian island of Sulawesi (Figures 0.1, 0.2). The shape of Sulawesi is poetically referred to by the playwright Louis Nowra as akin to an octopus caught in an electric blender. The southern peninsula of Sulawesi is home to the Bugis ethnic group. Bugis are renowned for their seafaring skills. Indeed, Bugis were once such feared pirates that sailors would warn their mates, "Beware of the Bugis man." As the legend goes, this grew into the saying, "Beware of the Boogie Man."

The topic of this book reveals another fascinating aspect of Bugis culture: gender multiplicity. The Bugis language, Basa Ugi, has five terms to describe an individual's gender identity: *makkunrai* (feminine woman), *oroané* (masculine man), *calalai* (masculine female), *calabai* (feminine male), and *bissu* (transgender shaman). These translations are very cursory and by no means reveal the depth of these subjectivities; it will take this book and more to explore the real richness of these multiple gender identities.

I first went to Indonesia during my freshman year at university. I immediately became interested in the issue of gender relations, although admittedly at that point my focus was on relations between women and men. It was not until I became a PhD candidate in 1998 that the possibility of multiple gender categories came to my attention. At the suggestion of my supervisors, I read a paragraph in Christian Pelras' book, *The Bugis,* that would excite any would-be gender researcher:

> One cannot conclude a discussion of gender among the Bugis without reference to the existence and importance of [a], as it were, third gender, the *calabai',* and a less well-known fourth one, the *calalai'.* The *calabai',* etymologically "false women," are male transvestites and the *calalai',* "false men," female ones. Very little has been written on this subject, apart from a little embarrassed explanation by Matthes (1872) and some recent research by

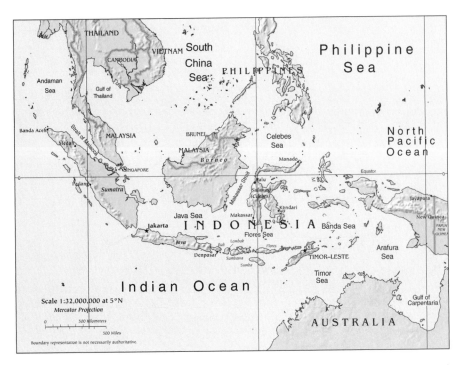

FIGURE 0.1 Map of Indonesia. Sulawesi is the octopus-like island near the center of the map.

Hamonic (1975; 1977a; 1987b; 40–48), since the allusion made by James Brooke in the journal of his visit to Wajo in 1840....(1996: 165)

Brooke noted in his journal:

The strangest custom I have observed is, that some men dress like women, and some women like men; not occasionally, but all their lives, devoting themselves to the occupations and pursuits of their adopted sex. In the case of the males, it seems that the parents of a boy, upon perceiving in him certain effeminacies of habit and appearance, are induced thereby to present him to one of the rajahs, by whom he is received. These youths often acquire much influence over their masters....(1848: 82–83)

Pelras's point that "[v]ery little has been written on this subject" immediately grabbed my attention, and I soon headed off to Sulawesi to learn more about this complex gender system. I hope that by recounting my experiences, observations, and conversations, I will help readers become aware of the multiplicity of gender identities in Bugis South Sulawesi. I also hope to enable readers to imagine subjectivities that are not constrained by dichotomous gender categories.

Dichotomous gender categories refer to the notion that there are only two gender identities, man and woman, and that these are in opposition to each other. Western thinking has long been based on the notion that there are two

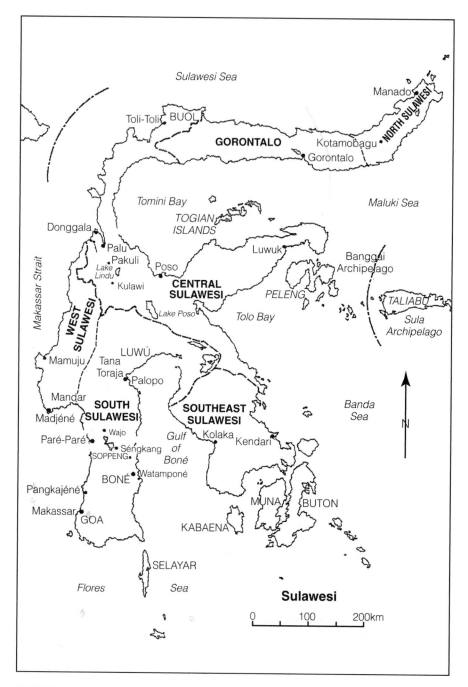

FIGURE 0.2   Map of Sulawesi, showing key South Sulawesi centers such as Sengkang, Soppeng, Paré Paré, Boné, and Makassar. Reprinted and updated with the kind permission of Greg Acciaioli.

biological sexes, female and male, on which are naturally based two genders, woman and man. This notion came to be dominant in Western thinking in the early eighteenth century, displacing the previous assumption that there were three biological sexes (male, female, intersexed) and a resulting two genders (Trumbach, 1994: 111). As a result of thinking in terms of gender dualisms, in the West we hear expressions such as, "I don't feel like a man, but I have a male body; therefore, I must be a woman trapped in a man's body." In other words, living in a society that acknowledges only two legitimate gender categories means that if you are not a man, you must therefore be a woman (Bolin, 1994). This case study reveals a different, and arguably more dynamic, way of thinking about gender.

The ethnography's first chapter is an introduction that tells of my first experiences of fieldwork, looking at issues of choosing a field site, acceptance into the community, and eliciting information. Chapter 1 also familiarizes readers with the location of the research, and it discusses methodological issues related to conducting research into gender and sexuality in Bugis society.

Chapter 2 opens by offering a vignette of a Bugis cultural festival. The chapter then moves on to a discussion of the concept of gender, asking two key questions: What does gender mean? What constitutes gender identity? *Gender* is a word frequently used in daily conversation, but often there is little understanding of what it encompasses. Indeed, *gender* is often erroneously considered to be a synonym for "woman." After discussing my initial understanding of gender, the chapter then looks at what the term means for people in South Sulawesi. How do Bugis understand gender? How is gender expressed? How do individuals see themselves becoming gendered individuals? This chapter endeavors to present a local understanding of gender and gender identity, showing that Bugis conceptualizations of gender are constituted by a multitude of variables and that the various combinations of these variables result in a number of different gender identities. For instance, in order to be a Bugis woman, an individual needs to not only be female but she should also feel, act, and dress like a woman. If she does not conform to these ideals, a female may be considered other than a woman. This understanding of Bugis gender enables consideration of more than two genders based on two anatomical sexes.

There is no indigenous word for gender in the Bugis language and, linguistically, gender is largely downplayed. For instance, siblings are referred to not by their sex (e.g., "brother" or "sister") but by their relative age (e.g., "elder sibling" or "younger sibling"). Chapter 3, then, examines several fundamental questions: Is gender an important concept in Bugis South Sulawesi? If gender is important, in what ways is it important? How is the significance of gender articulated? How does gender interact with other fundamental facets of Bugis society, such as status considerations, government discourses, and Islam?

Having established an understanding of what gender means and whether it is an important concept in Bugis society, the book moves to Chapter 4 to explore the subjectivities of individuals who are female-bodied but who do not consider themselves, nor are they considered, women. Rather these individuals are calalai. After examining why very few individuals identify as calalai, the chapter looks at ways in which some females contest womanhood and, in doing so, present forms of female masculinity. Included in this discussion is a look at community reactions to calalai.

Chapter 5 investigates ways in which some males contest images of ideal masculinity and present their own gendered identity, that of calabai. As with other chapters, key informants narrate their own experiences of gender, and in this way, readers get a sense of what it is like to be calabai. Society's perceptions of calabai, especially in respect to Islam, are also considered.

Chapter 6 provides insights into bissu (androgynous shaman) subjectivity and reveals ways in which gender considerations underpin bissu identity. Using ethnographic material, I examine the extent to which bissu derive their power from the belief that they are predifferentiated beings who embody a perfect combination of female and male elements (e.g., bissu have not yet divided to become either male or female but remain an amalgamation of both). In this chapter, I also assess rituals of becoming bissu and look at what is involved in the daily life of bissu. The roles and positions of bissu in Bugis and Islamic society are also addressed.

In Chapter 7, I recount two Bugis weddings to further examine issues of gender. Weddings reveal a great deal about the respective roles of bissu and calabai in Bugis society, and about general notions of gender. The first wedding I explore is a high-status wedding in Jakarta at which bissu officiated. The second wedding I explore is a low-status wedding in Sengkang at which calabai played a central role. By surveying these weddings, I show how bissu and calabai continue to undertake a recognized and essential role in Bugis society.

The book's final chapter draws the ethnography to a close, reiterating that gender in Bugis South Sulawesi is a multifarious concept and that more than two genders are possible.

ACKNOWLEDGMENTS

I first went to Indonesia in 1994. During this time, and particularly since I started research on gender in 1998, I have met many wonderful people to whom I am profoundly grateful. I would first like to thank people in South Sulawesi for their hospitality and acceptance—*saya bersyukur dan mengucapkan banyak terima kasih karena selama saya berada di Sulawesi Selatan banyak mendapat dukungan dan bantuan*: Puang Matoa Saidi, Haji Lacce', Haji Gandaria, Yanti, Karol, Soer, Acing, Andi Bau Muddaria Petta Balla Sari, Andi Hasan Mahmud, Andi Mappasissi, Andi Mappaganti, Drs. Muhlis, Dr. Dian Abdurachman, Pak Budi dan keluarganya, Professor Dharmawan Mas'ud, Dr. Nurul Ilmi Idrus, dan khusus Andi Idham Bachri dan keluarganya.

I want to especially thank Greg Acciaioli and Lyn Parker, to whom I am most indebted for their continuing encouragement and unfailing support. A special thank you to Evelyn Blackwood, Saskia Wieringa, Peter Jackson, Tom Boellstorff, Campbell Macknight, Veronica Strang, Roger Tol, Sirtjo Koolhof, Ian Caldwell,

Vicky Walters, Susanna Trnka, Kathryn Wellen, Linda Rae Bennett, Jen Avery, and Sue Warino is well deserved. I also want to acknowledge Lin Marshall, Janice Stockard, Sara Dovre Wudali, Leata Holloway, George Spindler, and the entire production team for their encouragement to publish in the Case Studies in Cultural Anthropology series and for their insightful editorial assistance.

Sponsorship and funding for my research has come from a number of sources, including Auckland University of Technology, the University of Western Australia (both from Asian Studies and Anthropology), the Australian National University, Hasanuddin University in Indonesia, the Indonesian Institute of Sciences (Lembaga Ilmu Pengetahuan Indonesia), the Dutch government, a Huygens Nuffic Fellowship, the Royal Institute of Linguistics and Anthropology (KITLV) in the Netherlands, National Geographic, AsiaPacifiQueer, the Sir Reginald Savory Fund, and the Asia:NZ Foundation.

I would like to thank the following publishers for allowing me to build on material in Chapters 2, 3, and 4 that appears elsewhere: *Intersections* (Graham, 2001); the *Journal of Gender Studies* (Graham, 2004a); the *Journal of Bisexuality* (Graham, 2004b); and edited collections by Blackwood and Wieringa (Davies, forthcoming[b]); Stephen Epstein (Davies, 2006[a]); and Vasilikie Demos (Davies, 2006[b]). This ethnography will be further elaborated on and incorporated into a more theoretical framework in a future publication with Routledge Curzon (Davies, forthcoming[a]).

Last but not least, I would like to thank my family: Mum, Dad, Jeannette, Chris, and their partners; my aunts, uncles, and cousins; Grandma, Pa, and Gran. Finally, a special thank you to my favorite critic, Tom Graham Davies, who has read this manuscript too many times to count and who makes my life such a joy.

1

Introduction: First Forays into Fieldwork

As the sun beat down ever more strongly, I began to wonder about the veracity of the information I had earlier received. I had arrived in Sengkang, a small town on the island of Sulawesi, the day before, fortuitously the day before Indonesia's National Day of Independence. Eager to explore, I quickly unloaded my pack and headed out from the guesthouse. Buying film supplies, I struck up a conversation with the couple who owned the shop. I told them about my intention to study notions of gender in the region. I also mentioned that I had heard there were various gendered identities in Sulawesi: women, men, **calalai, calabai,** and **bissu.**

At that preliminary stage of my fieldwork, I was not particularly familiar with the latter categories. In my understanding, calalai were females who performed many of the roles usually associated with men and who dressed like men. Conversely, calabai were males who performed many of the roles usually associated with women and who often dressed like women. Bissu were transgendered individuals who could be possessed by spirits in order to bestow blessings. While my interlocutors were not acquainted with calalai or bissu, they quickly pulled out some photos they had taken of a calabai beauty contest held the week before. "Now, if you want to meet calabai," the husband told me, "just come here tomorrow and you will see many calabai marching past."

No one was quite sure what time the marching would start, so early the next morning I breakfasted on fried rice and walked back into town. I went to the photo shop and was told to wait. Across from the photo shop was a small triangular piece of grass yet unoccupied. I moved there and unfurled my umbrella to provide welcomed shade. It was an interesting spot to sit. Sitting at the top of the main road, it provided a vantage point over the bustling market and the chaotic bus station. As it was still early, the fish section was thriving. The fishmongers were yelling out their specials: crab, lake fish, ocean fish, seashells, prawns, stingrays, dried fish. The fish section was under a cover, and the men were squatting on raised planks of wood and brushing away flies with banana-leaf fans. Potential buyers checked the freshness of the wares, inspecting the clarity of the eyes and the redness of the gills. Since it was so early, many of the fish were still thrashing about in the trays, and crabs were attempting to make stealthy escapes.

A little closer to where I sat was the fruit and vegetable section of the market. Women were walking up and down the aisles, occasionally carrying an armload of produce out to a pedicab and telling the driver to wait because there was more to come. If someone was buying for a celebration, a number of pedicabs were hired and, when full, were pedaled home by the drivers for a fee. The range of produce was immense: coconuts (young, old, dehusked, and crushed), durian, mango, pineapple, papaya, passion fruit, pomegranates, snake fruit, bananas, and mangosteen. Then there was the array of vegetables, spices, and other assorted produce.

Behind me was the bus station, a seething mass of people, goats, buses (large and small), cars, and motorbikes. There was no bitumen and the dust was choking. You could buy a ticket to any place in Sulawesi from there. The five-hour (200 km) trip to the capital city of Makassar cost as little as Rp20,000 (US$2), but you would have to share your seat with another person and often a chicken and a basket of dried fish. For enough money, you could even charter one of the cars to take you all the way to Manado in the far north. Around the bus station was a circle of small kiosks selling everything you could possibly need on your journey: cigarettes, matches, bottled water, dates, and for children, small rattling toys guaranteed to annoy adults.

Soon it was approaching noon and the sun was getting hotter. As fast as I drank water, it seemed to seep through my skin and soak my clothes. Finally, after midday prayers, the crowd lining the side of the road swelled to two and three deep. "*Sudah! Sudah!*" a child cried; the parade was starting. I looked up the road, away from the market, and even though I was staring into the sun, I could make out the shape of figures marching in procession down the road. As the figures neared, I saw that they were schoolchildren, impeccably dressed in their smart red-and-white (primary school) or blue-and-white (high school) uniforms. Some of the girls were wearing *jilbab,* the Islamic head veil. The children marched in orderly fashion past me. For forty minutes, children strode by, honoring the declaration of independence proclaimed more than half a century before. I had serious doubts that calabai would be marching in such a nationalistic parade.

Something soon caused the crowd to get excited. I shaded my eyes and looked at the crest of the hill. Marching girls! What took me by surprise was that the marching girls were wearing short, shiny miniskirts—a stark contrast to the veiled faces of some of the women surrounding me. I had spent almost a month in Sulawesi and had never seen a woman revealing her knees or shoulders, much less most of her thighs, in such an official and public celebration.

The marching girls were soon somewhat closer. The child who had first signaled the start of the parade looked up at me and said, "*Sudah, calabainya sudah datang* (It's time, the calabai have arrived)." About thirty calabai were marching, half from Sengkang and the remainder from the neighboring town of Palopo. Unlike the schoolchildren, who marched modestly and demurely, the calabai were outrageous and indecorous. Not only were they wearing tiny miniskirts in lurid colors, some with black boots, tight tank tops, and a copious amount of make-up, but their behavior was similarly extroverted. Instead of keeping their eyes averted, they seductively gazed at men and begged the men to flirt with them. Some calabai even approached men and bent over, shaking their bottoms at them. The marching routine included numerous dance steps. The one that received the most enthusiastic crowd reaction was called *"Variasi Nomor Tiga"* ("Variation Number Three"). It involved the whole troop moving in unison side-to-side and ended with extremely evocative pelvic thrusts (Figures 1.1, 1.2, 1.3).

FIGURE 1.1 Calabai marching in an Independence Day parade

F I G U R E 1.2 Calabai marching past a mosque in an Independence Day parade

F I G U R E 1.3 Calabai who have just marched in a parade

Myriad questions raced through my mind: Who were calabai? Why were they marching in this otherwise seemingly conservative nationalistic parade? Did they play a significant role in society? How did society in general react to calabai? How did someone become calabai? And what about the other categories, calalai and bissu? How did they fit into society? Could there be five gender categories? If so, what did this mean? Indeed, what did the concept of "gender" mean in South Sulawesi? Was it an important factor in daily life? How did its meaning inform gender identity? Still pondering these questions, I returned to the guesthouse impressed by the amount I had yet to learn about **Bugis** society. Convinced that gender would be a fascinating topic of research, when I arrived back in Australia some weeks later I immediately began preparations to return to Indonesia to start extensive fieldwork.

FIELD SITE

Sengkang is in the center of South Sulawesi, making access to other important locations relatively easy (Figure 1.4). The town has grown up on the shore of Danau Tempe, a huge lake in the middle of which is a floating village. One of my favorite pastimes during fieldwork was to board one of the dugout canoes

FIGURE 1.4 A view of Sengkang taken from the mosque

FIGURE 1.5   A man relaxing on his canoe

taking foodstuffs out to the floating houses (**bola monang,** B) and enjoy the hour-and-a-half journey past waterbirds and lake vegetation (Figure 1.5). We would arrive and be greeted with fresh fried bananas and the pungent smell of drying fish (Figure 1.6). Sometimes even the town of Sengkang itself became surrounded by water during floods, affirming the decision to build houses on stilts (Figure 1.7). At such times, the only way to get around was by boat (Figures 1.8, 1.9).

It was not just the aesthetic appeal of Sengkang that confirmed it as a good field site. Calabai play an active and highly visible role in local society, as revealed in the Independence Day parade, and people were always anxious to offer their opinions on calabai, some opinions more informed than others:

AUTHOR: Why are there so many calabai in Sengkang?

TUKANG BECAK: Oh, indeed there are many calabai in Sengkang.

AUTHOR: Why is this?

TUKANG BECAK: It's because people here eat a lot of fish heads (**kepala ikan**).

AUTHOR: Fish heads! Whatever do you mean?

TUKANG BECAK: Yeah, fish heads have lots of hormones (*hormon*) in them that cause you to become calabai.

Before embarking on fieldwork, I had to gain proper permission from Indonesian authorities to conduct research in South Sulawesi. With this permission in hand, I returned to Sulawesi in April 1999. While I had selected Sengkang as a field site, I did not head straight to Sengkang at this time because my language

FIGURE 1.6 Drying fish

FIGURE 1.7 A typical Bugis house on stilts (*bola riase'*)

FIGURE 1.8 The town of Sengkang after heavy rains

FIGURE 1.9 An overflowing river near Sengkang

skills needed attention. While my Indonesian was passable, my knowledge of Bugis was nonexistent. I moved into a **kos,** a small boarding house for students, on the campus of Hasanuddin University in Makassar and studied Bugis with Pak Muhlis. I chose to study with Pak Muhlis because he was a very able and patient teacher and also because he did not speak English. While I think my Bugis would have developed more quickly had I received instruction on issues like grammar in English rather than in a language I was not yet proficient in, I would have constantly spoken in English with Pak Muhlis, and my Indonesian would have suffered. As a result of this particular choice, my Indonesian improved in leaps and bounds, but my progress with Bugis was somewhat less impressive.

After two months of learning Bugis in Makassar, I relocated to Sengkang. While I initially planned to stay only temporarily with Puang Datu Petta Bala Sari, the arrangement turned out to be quite fortuitous. Puang Datu was one of the highest-ranking nobles in Sulawesi and was in effect the Queen of Wajo', the regency of which Sengkang is the capital. Because her family so frequently visited her, over time her residence grew and was eventually transformed into a guesthouse. Staying with Puang Datu and her family provided many opportunities, notably an invitation to the wedding of the daughter of the mayor of a district in Jakarta. Two bissu were summoned to attend this wedding, and I was able to travel with them and record their role in this royal event—I recount this wedding in Chapter 7. Sadly, though, Puang Datu passed away during the preparation of this book.

As a friend once told me, home is where your books are, and so home for me was Sengkang and Puang Datu's residence. I did, however, travel a great deal during my fieldwork. I would stay, for instance, in Sengkang for two weeks and then spend a week in Boné with Andi Mappassisi and his family. I would return to Sengkang for a further fortnight, then spend a week with Haji Gandaria in Paré Paré, or with Puang Matoa Saidi in Pangkep, or with Andi Idham Bachri and his family in Makassar. During the East Timor crisis, when Australians were increasingly viewed with suspicion, I relied on the hospitality of the Andersons at Patilla. I also traveled to Jakarta with Puang Datu and 300 other family members to attend the aforementioned wedding. All 300 of us were accommodated, fed, and entertained for an entire month at the Mayor's residence.

METHODOLOGY AND THE RESEARCH PROCESS

While the course of my fieldwork was rather serendipitous, I did employ an extended case-study methodology. I used a snowballing method to establish initial contacts and, while maintaining many of these and continuing to take advantage of further introductions, I became particularly close to just a few of these individuals and their families. These people were warm, welcoming, and encouraging of my research. They were also insightful and willing to share their thoughts and opinions, not just on matters of gender and sexuality but also on more general aspects of Bugis society. I was somewhat selective in the relationships I fostered because I wanted to become closely involved in the lives of calalai, calabai, and bissu. I also wanted to spend time in a number of different places in South Sulawesi.

Not everyone I met welcomed my research. Some people did not grasp the potential importance of such a study and dismissed my questions as trivial. Other people I spoke with were opposed outright to any research on variously gendered individuals. One university lecturer, for instance, bluntly told me to forget doing research on calabai because calabai are committing sins against humanity, and getting to know calabai would mean that I too was committing a sin. Only a small number of people ever expressed such sentiments, though.

I arrived in South Sulawesi wanting to understand more about how gender operates. I found the best way to do this was to take advantage of invitations directed my way and to observe and question daily life. Invitations were extended to such events as weddings, funerals, birth ceremonies, initiation rites, birthday parties, fashion parades, official government functions, spiritual rituals, and blessings. By attending these events and staying with my hosts, for anywhere from one night to one month, I was able gradually to increase my understanding of how gender comes into play in Bugis life. At each of these events I would be introduced to more people, and while concentrating on strengthening my relationship with a few key informants, I accepted as many invitations to other events as I could.

I studiously took notes of what I was witnessing, sometimes during events and conversations, sometimes soon after they had occurred. Notes were recorded in a mixture of English and Indonesian, depending on which language better expressed the idea. As time went on, the balance of English to Indonesian changed, and larger segments were recorded in Indonesian. Reading over some of my later field notes is a curious endeavor, and readers would find such puzzling sentences as "Yulia just went to *mencari cowok* saying that *dia pengeng cuci mata, ya ampun!" Pengen* is a colloquial Indonesian word meaning "to want something." However, until recently I was under the impression that the word was *pengeng,* as written in this field note excerpt. It was only when my Bugis friend and colleague Dr Nurul Ilmi Idrus was kindly proofreading this manuscript that I found out that *pengen* did not end with a "g." In Bugis, all words either end with a vowel or with "ng." Consequently, when many Bugis speakers are using Indonesian, they add the letter "g" to the end of many words, for instance, *makan* (eat) becomes *makang.* Indeed, if I am speaking in Indonesian, people can often tell that I learned the language in South Sulawesi because of my pronunciation and word use.

I tape-recorded some interviews, but most of the good information I obtained was so spontaneous that "hang on until I press play" would have destroyed the mood. During my write-up phase, a series of postgraduate writers' workshops were held at the University of Western Australia. This provided a great environment for students to present rough drafts of chapters. One of the comments that was raised in relation to a chapter I presented was that my informants sounded overly articulate. I then became very anxious about the fact that I had lost much of the nuance of the narratives. I started to think that perhaps I should have tape-recorded conversations to allow me to reproduce informant's words verbatim. To this end, I greatly admire the approach of Serena Nanda (1999) and Don Kulick (1998) to ethnography. My supervisors suggested I look at Clifford Geertz's (1976) work, and it was here that I found legitimization for my method. Geertz similarly took handwritten notes, rarely tape-recording conversations. While Geertz (1976: 385–386) acknowledges, "As a result of this method of work there is perhaps less verbatim material in the notes than in those cases where the anthropologist works with an interpreter and records...the text and its translation, or demands a 'literal' account from the interpreters," he believes that "whatever loss of accuracy is involved in non-verbatim translation it is more than compensated for in the increased quantity and variety of material one gets and the greater degree of naturalness and free-flow quality of the interview situation." While this is a debatable point, it is the way I found most appropriate.

Because of the nature of the context in which I pursued my research, I did not feel it necessary to prepare set questions or initiate a questionnaire or survey. Moreover, I rarely arranged for a formal interview to take place. My fieldwork consisted of one month of preliminary research (August, 1998), twelve months continuous fieldwork (April 1999–April 2000), and an additional eight months of periodic return, spaced between August 2000 and July 2005 (Figure 1.10).

FIGURE 1.10   The author with one of her Bugis host families

LANGUAGE

The information I gathered was primarily elicited and received in Indonesian. I did, however, persevere with learning the Bugis language, and indeed learning two new languages provided many laughs, usually at my expense. Spending a lot of my time with calabai, who are frequently referred to in Indonesian as *bencong*, I was often thinking about them. This included the time I asked my host-uncle if he would let me ride pillion (*bonceng*) to the market. What came out, however, was "*Boleh minta tolong Om, boleh dibencong ke pasar* (Uncle, could you transvestite me to the market)?" I had mistakenly substituted the word *bonceng* (to ride pillion) with *bencong* (transvestite/transgender male).

One evening, I did not have the stamina to sit up until midnight to watch the end of a Hindi movie. There would, of course, be another one on when I woke up in the morning. I excused myself, explaining that I was sleepy and wanted to go to bed. I had, however, recently learned a new word, which sounded frighteningly like the word for "sleepy." My excuse to want to go to bed (*ngantuk*) came out as *nyentot*. I had expressed a desire not to sleep but to *nyentot* (fuck). Everyone looked at me stunned, except my host-grandmother, who let out a small snicker, which grew and grew. Everyone soon followed suit, but for the rest of the year I always used the Bugis word *cakkaru'du'* (sleepy).

Despite all this, my Indonesian progressed well, and I was able to conduct reasonably fluent conversations and understand much of what was said. Even though I devoted time each day to learning Bugis—in addition to listening to the hour-long Bugis sermon that followed the 4:30 a.m. call to prayer—I did not attain proficiency in Bugis. I realized how little I was understanding when I finally became cognizant of the fact that the *imam* (prayer leader) was not constantly talking about calalai in his morning sermons but that he was actually saying *calalé* (myself).

If I conducted an interview or became involved in an in-depth conversation, the medium used was Indonesian. In situations where an informant did not speak Indonesian, someone close by would offer help with translations. Bissu have their own sacred language, Bahasa Bissu, which is also referred to as *Basa Toriolo* (Language of the Ancients), or *Bahasa Dewata* (Language of the Gods). Bissu were permitted to translate some of their chants and mantras; however, many are sacred, and it is forbidden for bissu to translate them without elaborate rituals being performed first. In cases where Bahasa Bissu could be translated, someone would provide an Indonesian translation.

I reproduce the words of my informants throughout this book, although all names are pseudonyms. I also employ the use of my own field notes, which are indented and rendered in italics. Indonesian words appear in italics with a translation when they first appear or when they have not appeared for a while. Bugis words are in italics and appear with a "B" and with a translation. The "B" follows the Bugis word, for instance, regalia (*arajang,* B), or *arajang* (B, regalia). The exceptions to this are calalai, calabai, and bissu, which, while Bugis words, are not so indicated due to their frequency and focality. Glottal stops, which occur frequently in Bugis, are signified by ': for instance, *siri'*.

There is much debate about whether to render foreign words in italics when writing in English. Some scholars argue that italicizing foreign words contributes to the process of Otherizing non-Western concepts. But the other side of the argument is that there is value in avoiding homogenizing diverse concepts and challenging readers' perceptions of issues dealing with gender and gender identity by showing, through italicization, that these are discrete concepts. Moreover, rendering words in italics can remind readers that a gendered identity, although labeled with a single term such as bissu, is not a homogenous group; numerous individual differences remain within such groups. In this ethnography, I have decided to italicize non-English words, with the exception of calalai, calabai, and bissu. I have refrained from italicizing the latter due to unresolved concerns over unduly Otherizing these identities.

As neither the Indonesian nor Bugis language distinguishes between gender pronouns, instead using the gender nonspecific third-person singular pronouns *dia* and *-i/na-/-na* respectively, I follow Blackwood (1998) and use *hir* and *s/he* to refer to calalai, calabai, and bissu. By using hir and s/he, I want to signify gender identities not based on moving from one normative gender to the other. While I acknowledge the symmetry imposed on calalai, calabai, and bissu by referring to them using the same pronominal conventions, I find this the most suitable way. While I could refer to calalai using *s/he* and *hem* and calabai using *s\he* and *hir,* this would suggest bissu be indicated by using *it* and *its,* which does not sit well. Moreover, multiple conventions may confuse rather than elucidate differences for readers and do not fully address the asymmetry problem that exists among these three categories.

I considered using **oroané** (B) and **makkunrai** (B) throughout this book to encourage readers to view the categories "man" and "woman" through emic eyes. I have decided against this, however, because I found that with the introduction of so many new terms and new ideas, the use of *makkunrai* and *oroané* added unnecessary confusion. I therefore use *woman* and *man,* but I stress here that while these categories correspond to general images of "woman" and "man" elsewhere, they are Bugis categories and thus are not perfectly translatable.

It is worth making clear here the distinction between such terms as *feminine* and *masculine.* In this book, I use *female* and *male* to refer to biological sex, acknowledging that female and male are social constructs. I use *woman* and *man* to refer to the social categories of female and male. *Feminine* and *masculine* are used to refer to types of behavior or appearance. For instance, tucking a sarong in at the waist is a feminine style while rolling a sarong down from the waist is a masculine style.

I also use others words in this book that may not be readily understandable. While I define such words more specifically within the main text of the book, I will just briefly outline a few of them here. *Heterogender* is a term I use to describe individuals who are of the same biological sex but who belong to different gender categories—a calabai–man relationship is seen by many Bugis as acceptable because it is a heterogender relationship. *Homogender* is a term I use to describe individuals who are of the same biological sex and who belong to the same gender category—a man–man romantic relationship is not given legitimate space in Bugis society because it is considered a homogender relationship. *Heteronormative* is a term used to convey the notion that a society considers heterosexuality and binary genders to be normal and all other sexualities and genders to be abnormal. I also use the ubiquitous term *Western*. This is a highly problematic term and it has attracted a litany of critique, but I find it helpful in juxtaposing certain situations and positions. So while recognizing that there is no singular entity that can be called "the West," I use it in this book as a heuristic device. I use *gender* to refer to the mix of biology, subjectivity, roles, behavior, and sexuality that combines in various ways to induce the development of an individual's gender identity. Finally, some people's names appear with the title **Andi,** which signifies high status, and **Puang,** which signifies royal status.

So let us turn now to gender in Bugis South Sulawesi.

2

This Thing Called Gender

INDEPENDENCE DAY: A PRELUDE

"Quick, hurry up (Ayo, cepat dong)!" *screeched Khadija, "We'll be late for the Bugis Pop Song Festival* (Festival Lagu Pop Bugis)." *I had just enough time to grab my bag before Khadija's arms seized my waist and she maneuvered me out the door. "Patience, patience* (sabarlah)," *I told her, but she was far too anxious to get going to be soothed. Despite my apparent reluctance, I too was keen to go, although perhaps for different reasons. Khadija wanted to "wash her eyes"* (cuci mata, *i.e., "check out" boys), while I wanted to see performances by bissu and calabai. It was almost the 17th of August, 1999, a year since my first trip to* **Sulawesi**, *and the town of* **Sengkang**, *like most towns throughout the nation, was celebrating Indonesia's Day of Independence. Khadija quickly roused the rest of the household, and we all made our way down the hill toward the bus station where the festival was being held. The bus station was a seething mass of people, the announcer claiming the audience was 10,000 strong. The first few performances involved women dressed in traditional Bugis clothing, singing songs of unrequited love. Next, a couple of groups of schoolgirls dressed in long Muslim gowns gave Islamic recitations (Figure 2.1). The following set consisted of men and women singing traditional Bugis songs. A pop band then came on, and the two young women singers were dressed in short black skirts, glittery tops, and knee-high boots. The men in the band were dressed in t-shirts and jeans. The gender of the next performer, though, I could not tell—why do I find it essential to attach a gender, or at least a sex, to people? The performer was dressed in a trendy black morning suit, and s/he had short hair that was shaved at the back. S/he walked onto the stage with a swaying, masculine gait. The facial features belied no femininity, although they were not harsh. S/he sang in a very high-pitched voice. I could not tell if s/he was female or male. The fact that this perplexed me so much revealed the importance I place on gender in ordering my world. Later in the evening when the winners were announced, the judges called the women up first. The person whose sex I could not determine won third place in the women's section. So s/he must be female, I thought, relieved at last to know the performer's sex. But why did s/he have no*

FIGURE 2.1   Girls performing Islamic songs at a local Bugis cultural festival

feminine markers like make-up, gold jewelry, pierced ears, or long hair? Gender ideals are so strict for women in Bugis society that it stuck me as surprising that such a masculine female was accepted so unquestioningly in a public nationalistic celebration. Perhaps Bugis society is more accepting of gender diversity than I had assumed. I turned to Khadija to see if she was surprised that this individual won a prize in the women's section; she was not. "S/he's calalai," Khadija informed me matter-of-factly, "so of course s/he must be like a man, but s/he has a female body so of course s/he competes with the women." The calalai timidly went on stage and collected the prize, then s/he went and sat with the other women, chatting and joking. (Field notes, 1999)

This festival occurred a year after my preliminary fieldwork trip to Sengkang and attending it made me realize that I was still grappling with this thing called *gender*. The successful performance by the calalai, whose name I never found out, gave me further insights into Bugis understandings of gender. It made me contemplate the strictness of gender versus gender fluidity, and it reminded me of an earlier experience that I will now recount.

Almost immediately after I arrived in South Sulawesi to begin my fieldwork in April 1999, I went with my Bugis language tutor to his family home in a small village about a five-hour motorbike ride from Makassar. The house was a simple stilt house (**bola riase'**, B) made of wood and bamboo. There was no fridge, no phone, no TV, and very little furniture. What struck me most, though, was how separate the sexes were. I never saw men and women socialize together; they sat

FIGURE 2.2 Calabai performing at a local Bugis cultural festival

in different parts of the house, ate at different times, and practically lived in separate worlds. After a week of staying there, I thought I had gender in that culture figured out—men are men, women are women, and never the twain shall meet. There was no gender fluidity in Bugis society, I thought. Genitalia determine gender, and gender determines when Bugis eat, where they sit, what games they play, and what skills they learn.

The Independence Day festival, and its inclusion of a calalai, made me think again about gender fluidity; and by *fluidity* I mean the lack of strict differences between women and men, and the ability of a female-bodied person to take on aspects of a man and vice versa. While biology never seemed to be forgotten (e.g., the calalai had to compete with the women), maybe the strictness of Bugis gender ideals meant that individuals who did not conform to strict gender types were seen as a different gender altogether. Did gender strictness, then, cause gender diversity? I was still pondering these questions when the next act of the festival started.

> It was the hooting and cajoling of the crowd that signaled that the calabai
> performance was about to start. Calabai did an outrageous performance. Not only
> were they wearing short skirts, body-hugging tops, and heavy make-up but also
> their parody of traditional Bugis dances was highly alarming to many Bugis elders,
> although hilarious to others (Figure 2.2). Their over-the-top femininity did not
> reflect conventional Bugis female gender ideals, and they certainly were not
> performing Bugis masculinity. Rather, through their performance, calabai
> reinforced their separate gender status. After the rousing calabai act, bissu came on

stage and shared with us their sacred dances and chants, although as these were for show and not for real, some essential elements were left out to ensure that the spiritual role of bissu was not devalued. The bissu performance signaled the end of the festival. Khadija had "washed her eyes," and I had seen performances by five different gendered identities: calalai, calabai, bissu, women, and men. But am I any clearer on this thing called gender? (Field notes, 1999)

THOUGHTS ON GENDER

My Initial Thoughts on Gender

So what is this thing called gender and how does it contribute to the formation of a gendered identity? When I first went to Indonesia, I was quite certain I had a fair idea. I knew that the English word *gender* derived from the Latin *genus,* which means "kind, sort, class." I also knew that for a long time in Western thought gender was assumed to be the natural outcome of biological sex. With this thinking, it was assumed that men were aggressive and women were nurturing, not because of the society in which they were raised but purely because of biology. In this view, there was no point in separating "natural" sex roles and behaviors from "constructed" ones.

I also knew that this view of biology causing gender had been superseded in Western theories and that the society in which people are born in large part constructs their gender. I was born in a society where girls wear pink and boys wear blue. Indeed, my brother and his partner have just had a baby. Because they were expecting a girl, my brother decorated the baby's room in a lovely peachy-pink color. As I type this, though, my brother is busily repainting the baby's room because, much to everyone's surprise, they had a boy. There is nothing essential about a baby boy having a blue bedroom, but the particular society in which my nephew Mitchell has been born suggests that boys should not sleep in pink-colored rooms. If he were born somewhere else, of course, this might be perfectly acceptable.

One of the first scholars to write about the social construction of gender was Margaret Mead (1935), an anthropologist who did extensive fieldwork in the Pacific regions. Mead suggested that gender was not just the result of biology but rather that gender was culturally produced. Mead even suggested that biology played a very small part in the construction of gender.

Before I started my fieldwork, I also made sure that I was aware of the work of other theorists who suggested that the link between gender and biology was weak. Simone de Beauvoir (1947), for instance, dismissed the idea of biological determinism underpinning gender.

I was also familiar with other important work on gender, such as that conducted by Sherry Ortner and Harriet Whitehead (1981), who identified a systematic way that culture produces gender. When speaking of gender, Whitehead (1981: 83) refers to the ideals that "give social meaning to physical differences between the sexes, rendering two biological classes, male and female, into two social classes, men and women."

More recently, Judith Butler (1990, 1993) has questioned the "materiality" of the body and suggested that the body is habituated to performing gender. In effect, the body only becomes real when we look at the gendered society in which it is constructed.

When I commenced fieldwork, I was thus dismissive of essentialist arguments that suggested there was something innate about gender. I thought that the body played an insignificant role in gender formation. I considered that gender was primarily a social construct, and I held fast to de Beauvoir's adage, "One is not born, but rather becomes, a woman." I also minimized the influence other factors could have on gender. I thought issues like sexuality, spirituality, roles, and occupation were not important considerations in becoming a gendered being.

Before beginning fieldwork, I had never really given much thought to the possibility of more than two genders, and certainly not to fourth and fifth gender identities. My thinking was mostly limited to people born in the "wrong body," for example, transgendered and transsexual individuals. While I had read Will Roscoe's (1991, 1998) work on gender variance among Native North American cultures, Serena Nanda's (1999) ethnography on *hijra* in India, and Gilbert Herdt's (1994) *Third Sex, Third Gender* anthology, among others, this work was limited to possible third-gender identities, and they did not really explore societies with four or more genders.

So my preliminary view of gender was that gender was based on two sexes (female and male), that a society constructs ideals based on these two sexes (feminine and masculine), and that this results in two socially constructed genders (woman and man). Once I arrived in Sulawesi, however, I had to revise this view.

Gender among Bugis

This chapter uses ethnographic material to show the particular way in which gender is viewed among Bugis I lived with in South Sulawesi. This view of gender will be primarily illustrated by revealing what constituents combine in the formation of a gendered identity. Before moving on to this, however, I want to add one particular caveat. The view I will share of gender is mediated by my own understanding, and it stems from the conversations I had with many, but certainly not with all, Bugis people. While I have shared my interpretation of Bugis gender with Bugis friends and colleagues, and they have affirmed my understanding, this book is still merely one person's particular view of Bugis gender.

There is no indigenous word for gender in the Bugis or Indonesian languages. Sometimes people use a derivation of the English word *gender,* or *jender.* Other times, people use *jenis kelamin* (type of sex organ), and while this refers to biological sex, it often represents notions of gender. The fact that there is no indigenous word certainly does not mean that the concept of gender is unimportant; Chapter 3 shows that gender is indeed an important concept in Bugis society. What it does mean, though, is that the notion of gender is expressed in ways other than with a single word. To begin with, I found this very problematic. It was not until I had been in South Sulawesi for a number of months that I started to see how gender is viewed. For many Bugis, numerous factors go into constituting an individual's gendered identity. One analogy presented to me was that of a cake (*kue*). When we look at a cake, we see something delicious and edible. But if we want to understand the cake and how it was made, we need to know what goes into it. But the ingredients—flour, eggs, butter, sugar—are not often eaten on their own. As such, in order to appreciate the cake, we need to see all the ingredients mixed together and baked. We can also apply this approach to people and gender. If we want to know what makes up a person's gender, then we need to look at all the separate parts, but in order to appreciate the whole person, we should not lose sight of the finished product. So what are all these parts that come together to form an individual's gendered identity? The body is certainly a major influence, and so I will start with a discussion of how ideas of the body help constitute a person's gender in Bugis society.

GENDERED BODIES

Eri

Eri was born in 1980 into a strict Muslim family living in a small town not far from Sengkang. Eri is the second of three daughters, and this environment ensured that s/he was aware of the ways in which girls ought to act. For Eri, though, the aspects associated with being born female—acting demurely, having long hair, cooking family meals—never seemed to suit hir temperament. This clash of ideas between Eri and hir parents and sisters meant that as soon as s/he could, Eri moved away from hir family home and began to behave in ways with which s/he was more comfortable. Now grown-up, Eri has reunited with hir family and, while hir parents are not happy that s/he is calalai, they have accepted hir gender.

Eri almost always dresses like a man. S/he wears trousers, shirts, and t-shirts. S/he has short hair. S/he is attracted to feminine women, and s/he works in the capital city of South Sulawesi, Makassar, as a disk jockey. While Eri certainly does not feel hirself to be a woman, s/he does not deny the fact that s/he is female-bodied.

Being Muslim, Eri has to go to the mosque to pray on occasion. In the mosque, men and women pray separately, and it is here that sex is the most important definer of individual identity. When I asked Eri about where s/he prays, with the women or with the men, s/he retorted that of course s/he must pray with the women because s/he is, after all, female. So no matter how much Eri may become like a man and how much s/he rejects being a woman, hir female body is never dismissed, neither by hirself nor by others.

Rani

Rani is a farmer who lives in a large village a couple of hours' drive north of Makassar. Rani lives with hir (unofficial) wife, Sia, and their adopted son.

I often stayed at Rani's house during my fieldwork both because Rani and Sia were very welcoming and because Rani is one of the few calalai I have met who has established an integrated role within hir home community.

Rani and Sia's house is small, consisting of a concrete slab partly covered with vinyl, a tin roof, and four small rooms (two bedrooms, a lounge, and a kitchen). There is an outdoor squat toilet, which is shared with no less than three cats who have taken up residence there, and a well from which water is drawn for washing and, after boiling, for drinking. The well is also used for bathing, and while it is partly enclosed with a bamboo fence, the wearing of a *sarong* is recommended.

Whenever I stayed with Rani and Sia, I was always given my own room. While I felt uncomfortable with this level of hospitality, especially knowing that the assorted nieces and nephews who often stay with Rani and Sia were forced to spend the nights with neighbors, my efforts at protesting were futile. Acts of generosity like this made me aware of my perceived position of relative power and made me question the deference with which I was treated. While I was only a twenty-four-year-old female student, which would not normally have attracted much status, I was from a rich Western nation and was accorded certain unearned privileges. I wonder still how Rani would be treated if s/he came to the West to conduct fieldwork—would anyone open their home to hir as warmly as s/he had opened hirs to me?

Early one afternoon, Rani and I were sitting on a wooden bench in the lounge room talking about Islam. A comment Rani made reveals the importance s/he and others place on the body. Like Eri, Rani noted that when s/he goes to the mosque to pray, s/he must pray as a female, even if s/he has been working in the rice fields alongside men all day. If s/he does not pray as a female, Rani believes that Allah will not acknowledge hir and therefore will not listen to hir prayers. For Rani, the body remains a fundamental definer of gender.

Yulia

Yulia was born male, although people unaccustomed to Bugis gender may easily assume s/he is female. S/he wears skirts and dresses, applies make-up, and has long hair. Even though s/he is closely aligned with images of popular forms of Bugis and Western femininity, hir body is not forgotten. Even Yulia hirself never forgets that s/he was born male.

Yulia works as an ***Indo' Botting,*** a term that translates as "Wedding Mother." An *Indo' Botting* is someone, either a calabai or a woman, who arranges all aspects of a wedding. *Indo' Botting* select the bridal attire, organize the food and seating arrangements, help the bride get dressed on the day of the wedding, and do the bride's hair and make-up—I explore the role of *Indo' Botting* more in Chapter 7. I often accompanied Yulia to weddings, and from hir I learned a great deal about gender through the ritual of marriage.

One evening I was helping Yulia get ready for a wedding, and while we worked we talked about how glamorous the bride would look. I asked Yulia what s/he would wear if s/he were getting married. Yulia responded that before such a special day came, s/he would like to get surgery to feminize hir body. S/he would like to get many things done; particularly she would like to get silicon injected into hir cheeks and lips to make them more feminine. Yulia acknowledged, however, that such procedures would not change the fact that s/he is male. S/he noted somewhat remorsefully that no matter how much silicone s/he gets injected or how much surgery s/he has, s/he will always be seen as male because of hir Adam's apple. Calabai can get breast implants and have their penis changed into a vagina, s/he commented, but they can never get rid of their Adam's apple. Calabai, according to Yulia, will always remain male.

Through these remarks, Yulia reveals the crucial role that biology plays in gender identity. However, I never heard from Yulia, or from anyone else, the notion of being trapped in the wrong body. Yulia believes that Allah made all human beings, and if calabai like hir have a male body and a feminine type of behavior, then this must be how Allah intended them to be. With this understanding, it does not make sense to explain gender diversity through the notion of individuals being caught in the wrong body, although many calabai still wish to feminize their appearance.

Ways That Gender Is Embodied

During my fieldwork, I was fortunate to have many long conversations with a respected Bugis man named **Pak** Hidya. One day we were talking about the body as a concept. I asked him how he thought the body was constituted and how all of the different gender identities in Bugis South Sulawesi fit into the larger gender picture. Pak Hidya picked up a stick and drew a line in the dirt. He pointed to one end of the line and said that real (*asli*) women are there, and then he pointed to the other end of the line and said that real men are there. Pak Hidya then pointed to various spots along the line, showing me where calalai, calabai, and bissu are respectively located. Calalai, calabai, and bissu, he revealed, are positioned between women who are at one extreme end and men who are at the other extreme end. The reason for the different locations, according to Pak Hidya, is the fact that different gendered identities have different natures (**sifat**).

For Pak Hidya, people are ordered along a horizontal line primarily according to their biological sex and then secondarily according to their behaviors. So, first along the line are female-feminine women (*makkunrai*, B). Next come calalai because they are female, but they have some male attributes. In the middle of the line are bissu because they embody a perfect combination of female and male elements. Next are calabai, who are male but who have some female attributes. At the other end of the line are male-masculine men (*oroané*, B).

Some people I spoke with found Pak Hidya's conceptualization of Bugis gender somewhat problematic. These people did not think that individuals can be ordered along such a straight line. Instead, they suggested that when drawing a conceptual map of Bugis gender, calabai should be placed closer to women than to men, and calalai should be placed closer to men than to women. Bissu, these people noted, are spiritual beings, so they cannot possibly be placed on a straight line next to mere mortals. Whereas Pak Hidya's conceptualization of gender privileged biological sex as the primary determinant of gender position-ing, these people suggested scattering gendered identities within a triangular con-ceptualization, with bissu at the apex and other gendered identities spread out below.

In grappling with conceptualizing gender and bodies, some people told me that the body and its relationship to gender should be expressed as complementary combinations of female and male. On this topic, I spoke with a local Islamic leader, Pak Rudin, who hinted of calalai being both female and male. He revealed that they are calalai because of physiology (*fisiologi*). While they are female-bodied, Pak Rudin asserted that calalai are not like other women internally and that in fact calalai have some male aspects. In effect, calalai combine both female and male attributes.

During another conversation, a Bugis man of noble descent, named Puang Nasah, told me that calabai are not men (*bukan laki-laki*) but their genitalia (*kelamin*) is male, and as such, they have a different genetic make-up from men. Drawing on his knowledge of human chromosomes, Pak Nasah pondered that maybe calabai have XXY chromosomes, unlike men who have XY, although if a particular calabai was more female than male, perhaps that individual would have XYY chromosomes.

Unlike Pak Hidya, Pak Rudin and Puang Nasah present an understanding of gender and the composition of the body in a way that accommodates androgyny. Bissu are beings who are considered to embody perfect combinations of female and male elements; this combination results in their superhuman power. The abil-ity to think in terms of complementary sexes, and combinations of male and female elements, as expressed by Pak Rudin and Puang Nasah, makes it possible to imagine multiple genders. This conceptualization of embodied gender also means that ideas such as being trapped in the wrong body do not make sense. While biology does not determine gender (e.g., females are not necessarily women), the body is very important in Bugis considerations of gender (e.g., a female can never be a man). Furthermore, for many people, there are not just two sexes; people can embody different amounts of female and male elements, thus allowing for the prospect of various genders.

FATE, SPIRIT, AND THE X FACTOR

Bodies are not the only factor contributing to gender and thus gender identity in Bugis South Sulawesi. For many people I spoke with, notions of spirituality were highlighted as key constituents of gender identity. Bugis are often cited as one of the most Islamic of all peoples in the Indonesian archipelago, so it comes as no surprise that fate, spirit and the X factor are important factors in gender formation.

Leena lives in a small village and s/he is a devout Muslim. S/he believes s/he is calalai because of God's (*Tuhan*) plan. God has a plan for all of us, s/he told me, and we are unable to resist it. Leena also talked about fate (**kodrat**) and said that if your *kodrat* is to be calalai, you have no option but to be calalai because people must follow their own *kodrat.*

In a similar vein, a middle-aged calabai named Andi Tenri, who lives in rural South Sulawesi, affirmed that for hir to be calabai is part of God's plan. It is hir *kodrat,* and Andi Tenri believes that at one point or another everyone's *kodrat* must appear (**muncul**) and the real person must come out.

Andu, another calabai, shared comparable thoughts, revealing that s/he is calabai because this destiny (**nasib**) was given to hir by Allah. During my conversation with Andu, Andu's mother came and sat with us, adding that she never wished for a calabai child, but there was little she could do, as it was Allah's will.

Andi Enni, a middle-aged calabai, disclosed that s/he came to be calabai from birth. Then, as s/he got older, hir identity continued to develop, and s/he started doing everything like a girl, for instance, playing with girls' toys. Andi Enni believes that for hir to be calabai is a *kodrat* given by Allah. Although Andi Enni did not really want this life, it is Allah's will; therefore, Andi Enni believes s/he must surrender to hir fate. At first, Andi Enni's parents were angry at hir for being calabai, but after a while, when s/he started to earn a good income, hir parents could not be angry with hir any longer. In any case, Andi Enni noted, how can you alter your *kodrat?*

There are, of course, many opinions within Bugis society, and some people do not think that *kodrat* is permanent. Even if calabai say they are calabai because they have a certain *kodrat,* some people told me that in fact calabai can change their *kodrat.* **Haji** Mulyadi, an *imam* (originally an Arabic word meaning "Muslim leader" or "prayer leader"), believes just this. He once told me that according to calabai, they believe it is their *kodrat* to be calabai, but they only say that because it is their hobby (*hobi*). Because it is a *hobi,* Haji Mulyadi believes calabai can change their gender identity. One example Haji Mulyadi offered of calabai changing their nature was of calabai fathering children. For Haji Mulyadi, the fact that some calabai can become sexually aroused by women, or at least have procreative sex with women, proves that their inner nature can change (*sifat bisa berubah*). Certainly their dominant nature is that of a woman, Haji Mulyadi conceded, but there *is* a "way out"; for instance, Haji Mulyadi believes calabai who sexually desire men should undergo sex-reassignment surgery (*berubah kelaminannya,* literally "change their genitals"). However, I never heard any calabai, calalai, or bissu positing that their *kodrat* could be altered.

Some people I talked with mentioned that gender identity is caused by having a particular spirit (*jiwa*). Chatting with Cappa' one evening as s/he waited for hir turn to DJ at a nightclub in Makassar, I asked hir why s/he identifies as calalai. S/he attributes hir gender identity to the particular *jiwa* s/he has. Tilly, a calabai, also used the term *jiwa* in respect to hir gender, saying that in order to be calabai, an individual must have the *jiwa* calabai.

Other people used the term **roh** (soul) to explain the acquisition of gender identity. For instance, Haji Mappaganti, a calabai who is employed as a primary school teacher, said that s/he knew from when s/he was really young that s/he would be calabai. When s/he was young, hir girlish behavior made hir parents very angry, and they would hit hir and try to get hir to be more like a boy. This punishment did not work because Haji Mappaganti is like s/he is because s/he has a particular *roh,* which, according to Haji Mappaganti, cannot be changed.

Some people found it hard to articulate what actually led them to assume their gender identity. In such instances, people occasionally used the term *faktor X* (the X factor). Maman, a calalai who works as a blacksmith, told me that hir parents really wanted a son, so s/he was treated like a boy. For Maman, becoming calalai was because of hir parents', especially hir father's, influence and also because of what s/he calls *faktor X.* Maman used *faktor X* as a way of expressing an unknown quality that encouraged hir to assume a nonnormative gender identity.

So we see that individuals describe and justify their gender identity using many different techniques. When individuals realize that their particular body type does not suit the ways in which they dress, behave, and act, they find ways of justifying their particular gender identity. Notions of fate, destiny, spirit, soul, and *faktor X* are used in this respect.

PLAYING OUT GENDER

Gender is not just about your body or about how you feel; for many Bugis, gender and gender identity are very much about what is performed in public. For instance, a person cannot merely decide to be calalai, because calalai have to act and dress as calalai.

Rani, who was introduced previously, is female-bodied, yet s/he is more like a man than a woman in most ways. S/he wears trousers or, if wearing a *sarong,* ties it like a man (rolled down rather than tucked in, like a woman would). Hir hair is cropped short. S/he uses swear words, smokes cigarettes, and walks alone at night. Rani also works alongside men in the rice fields. As mentioned earlier, Rani is married, although unofficially, to Sia, and they have adopted a son who calls Rani **Bapak** (Father). Even though Rani is female-bodied, s/he enacts particular behaviors to affirm hir identity as a masculine female, a calalai. Rani's desire to pursue these masculine actions confirms for hir and others that s/he is calalai.

I was told by some people that gender identity is caused by how you act. Idi, a 30 year-old man, stated that even though his friend was forced to marry a woman, his friend is still calabai because of how s/he acts. Haji Mulyadi told me that you can tell a calabai by how s/he acts. For instance, Haji Mulyadi said that his friend Haji Baco' was showing signs of being calabai while they were still at school. In Haji Mulyadi's understanding, the way that Haji Baco' acts in large part constitutes hir gender identity.

Some people talked about how Bugis gender identity is determined by exhibiting a mixture of normative behaviors of both women and men. A man of about 30, named Jero', told me that there are many different types of calabai and moreover that calabai have many different moods. Jero' then said that a calabai might be walking down the street with a swaying and exaggerated gait but that if a man came up and started harassing hir, s/he would quickly become more masculine and maybe even raise hir fists to fight. If calabai need to protect themselves, Jero' believes that they will draw on their masculine side.

Puang Sulai, a high-ranking nobleman introduced earlier, believes that calabai are amazing (*hebat*). Puang Sulai gave the example of Fitri, a local schoolteacher who goes to work wearing trousers. At school, Fitri is very strict with all the children, and s/he even yells at them. Then when Fitri comes home, Puang Sulai said that s/he takes off hir trousers, puts on a skirt and make-up, and becomes demure and soft in hir behaviors and mannerisms. In this way, Fitri is seen to embody both feminine and masculine behaviors.

How a person dresses also contributes to a person's gender identity in Bugis South Sulawesi. Ance', a calalai with a daughter, told me that a primary reason why s/he is calalai is because s/he hates women's clothing due to the fact that it is too restrictive. As a result, Ance' never wears **baju bodo** (traditional blouse) or **kebaya** (traditional Malay dress). By refusing to wear women's clothes and dressing like a man, Ance' publicizes hir masculine identity.

Santi also uses clothing to signal hir gender identity. Santi's favorite item of clothing is the miniskirt. While in some countries it is not uncommon for a woman to wear a miniskirt, in Bugis South Sulawesi it is exceptional for women to do this. As such, when Santi wears a miniskirt, s/he is signaling hir calabai identity.

Bissu also signal their gender identity in part through clothing. When they are performing ritual blessings, bissu wear a combination of feminine and masculine symbols. For instance, bissu may wear flowers—a feminine symbol—and carry a **keris** knife, a masculine symbol. Combining these accoutrements signals that bissu are a combination of male and female elements.

In developing a gender identity, the roles people perform, the behaviors people exhibit, the occupations people pursue, and the ways in which people dress all contribute to the formation of a gendered identity and to notions of what gender means among Bugis. As such, when we think of gender in Bugis South Sulawesi, we have to take all of these factors into consideration.

EROTIC DESIRE

Sexuality is a key aspect in the development of gender identity in Bugis South Sulawesi. What I mean by sexuality is the combination of erotic desire, whom individuals have sex with, and the roles they play in sexual encounters. Sometimes sexuality is used as a way of legitimizing a gender identity. Same-sex heterogender relationships are more openly acknowledged in Bugis society than same-sex homogender relationships. I use the phrase *same-sex heterogender relationship* here to describe a couple where both individuals are either male or female but where each of the respective partners is of a different gender, such as a relationship between a calalai and a woman. Conversely, I use the phrase *same-sex homogender relationship* to describe a couple where both individuals are either male or female but where each of the respective partners is of the same gender, such as a relationship between two men. As homogender romantic relationships tend not to be publicly acknowledged in South Sulawesi, particularly outside the metropolis of Makassar, if an individual has same-sex sexual desires, s/he may feel compelled to assume a different gender identity from hir partner. Moreover, an individual who takes on nonnormative gender attributes may wish to substantiate hir identity through involvement in a same-sex romantic relationship. It is important then to examine the influences of sexuality on the formation of gender identities in Bugis South Sulawesi.

Yanti is a calabai in hir 30s who told me that sexual awakening induced the development of hir gender identity. When s/he was in hir early 20s, Yanti had a girlfriend, but whenever they kissed, Yanti said there was no spark and it was like kissing a sister. When Yanti's marriage to a woman was arranged, s/he felt compelled to really think about hir sexuality. Yanti knew that s/he had always been attracted to men, but up to that point it was just a platonic attraction. Before s/he got married, Yanti felt that s/he had to know if s/he was sexually attracted to men; otherwise, it would not be fair to hir wife. So Yanti kissed a man, eager to see how it felt. As soon as their lips touched, Yanti knew that s/he was sexually attracted to him, and for hir this meant that s/he was calabai and that s/he could not marry a woman.

A friend of Yanti, named Yulia, also attributes sexual awakening in part to the development of hir gender identity. Like Yanti, it was when Yulia's marriage was arranged that s/he felt s/he needed clarification on hir sexuality. Yulia therefore had sex with a man to find out if s/he liked it, which s/he did. Yulia then refused to marry the woman hir family had selected. As Yulia's family is a part of the nobility (**bangsawan**), the shame Yulia felt at not conforming to the expectations hir family had of hir becoming a husband and father was great. Yulia felt s/he had no option but to leave hir hometown. We see here how status considerations can also influence a person's experience of gender—I discuss status in more depth in Chapter 3.

Like Yanti and Yulia, many calalai also see sexual desire as an important aspect of gender formation. When Eri was sixteen, a woman started paying hir a lot of attention, taking hir to the movies, and buying hir presents. Eri had grown up in a rough household and had felt unloved. The attention Eri received from this woman made hir feel wanted for the first time. Soon a physical relationship developed between them, and Eri said it was at this point that s/he became ill (*sakit*). Eri uses the word *sakit* to describe the point at which s/he developed same-sex sexual desire because like an illness, sexual desire is neither something you choose to get nor something you can necessarily cure.

Sexuality is for many Bugis intimately linked to gender identity. Indeed, if a calabai, for instance, erotically desires women, then s/he may be considered a fake calabai (calalai *palsu*). During a conversation with a devoutly Muslim calabai, named Haji Mappaganti, I was told that there are many different types of calabai. There are calabai whose grooming (**dandan**) is like that of women and who are attracted to men. It is these calabai that Haji Mappaganti believes are authentic (**asli**). Haji Mappaganti noted, however, that sometimes their *dandan* can be like that of a man, but they may still be sexually attracted to men. In this case,

Haji Mappaganti considers that they are still calabai because they may have been forbidden to dress like a woman by their parents. In illustrating this, Haji Mappaganti used the example of hirself. When s/he finished high school, Haji Mappaganti's *dandan* was like a woman, but hir parents desperately wanted hir to marry heterosexually. But Haji Mappaganti could not marry because s/he could not bear the thought of being sexually involved with a woman. So Haji Mappaganti ran away. Some time later, hir parents wrote hir a letter stating that it did not matter what type of person s/he was, they just wanted hir to come home. Haji Mappaganti did come home, but s/he knew s/he would have to wear men's clothing because s/he had just been on the pilgrimage to Mecca. Haji Mappaganti still had no sexual interest in women, though, and as such maintains that even though s/he dresses as a man, s/he is not attracted to women and therefore is still a calabai *asli*.

It is not just sexual desire that helps form gender identity in Bugis South Sulawesi; the roles a person plays in sexual relationships are also important considerations. Dilah, a calalai, noted that calalai do not want to be sexually entered (**dimasuki**). Rather, Dilah believes it is the role of calalai to enter their partners. For Dilah, women are sexually entered, so one way in which Dilah differentiates hirself from women is by being the one who enters hir partner.

Yulia told me that men do not want to be entered sexually; rather, men want to sexually enter calabai. If Yulia entered hir male partner, s/he considers that to be lesbian. The use of the term *lesbian* by Yulia suggests that for hir, while calabai–man relationships are between two opposites (a heterogender relationship), calabai–calabai relationships are between two same-gendered people (a homogender relationship), which is not particularly accepted in Bugis society.

There is a link in Bugis South Sulawesi between sexual role and gender, but this link is not always clear. In the capital city of Makassar, Takrim, a 30-year-old man, told me that increasingly, men who seek the services of calabai sex workers are requesting to be fucked (*dibo'ol*) by calabai or to perform fellatio on calabai. These men, though, are still conceptualized as men. So being sexually entered does not mean an individual is necessarily feminized. Perhaps part of the reason why being sexually entered does not necessarily threaten a man's masculinity is that it is not sexuality alone that determines a person's gender identity in Bugis South Sulawesi. Indeed, even sexual activity is not essential in forming a person's gender identity. Eka, for instance, lays claim to hir calabai identity not through sexual performance but through erotic desire. While Eka has never had a boyfriend, s/he desires men and this contributes to hir being calabai.

Sexual potency is sometimes taken into consideration in terms of Bugis gender identity. I was told by Wawal, a former calabai, that when he fathered a baby girl, he was therefore proved a man and could no longer be calabai. Usually, though, fathering children is not enough to render a calabai a man as some calabai have fathered children and are still considered calabai.

As can be seen, the relationship between sexuality and gender is anything but rigid. While sexuality contributes and, in some cases, confirms gender identity, it does not on its own determine gender identity in Bugis South Sulawesi.

CONCLUSION

This chapter has looked at Bugis conceptualizations of gender and gender identity. What the selected narratives show is that gender in Bugis South Sulawesi is a complex concept. This view of Bugis gender differs from other conceptualizations of gender throughout the world, and it defies many dominant gender theories. Bugis do not generally regard gender as something entirely essential and innate or as something entirely socially constructed; gender is in part constituted through both of these factors. Bugis gender is not thought to derive just from biology (particularly genitalia), from the work a person does, from the roles a person plays, or from a person's behavior; Bugis gender results in part from a combination of all of these factors. Bugis gender is not entirely underpinned by sexuality, but sexuality is significant. Bugis gender is not separate from notions of fate and destiny; these factors are part of the whole picture. Bugis gender is not assumed to merely refer to women and men; for many Bugis, gender also includes the categories of calalai, calabai, and bissu.

Bugis conceptualizations of gender are thus complex and take into account many factors. This understanding of gender fosters a system where gender multiplicity is accommodated. As the identities of calalai, calabai, and bissu show, in Bugis South Sulawesi it is necessary to think beyond a dichotomous construction of gender. Only with an emic understanding of gender can we appreciate Bugis gendered subjectivities. We move now to the incorporation of this understanding of gender and gender identity into an analysis of the importance and centrality of gender in Bugis South Sulawesi.

3

The Importance of Being Gendered

Is gender an important concept in Bugis society? Much of this book is predicated on an affirmative answer to this question. If gender is not a central consideration in Bugis South Sulawesi, then there is not much point in writing a book about it. It is easy to assume that gender is an essential factor in Bugis society simply because gender is significant in one way or another everywhere in the world. But of course we cannot just take this for granted.[1]

This chapter explores whether gender is an important consideration in Bugis society and if so, in what ways. In order to assess the centrality or otherwise of gender, I look at Bugis notions of social status. This chapter also reveals ideal gender types. In doing this, I first explore Bugis notions of shame to illustrate local gender ideals. I then examine gender ideals as presented by the Indonesian government, before moving on to analyse what Islam expects of individuals in terms of gender ideals. This chapter aims to present ideal gender models that people in Bugis South Sulawesi are encouraged to emulate. Of course, in everyday life local, national and religious gender norms are not easily disentangled and often become conflated in the development of an individual's gender identity. In later chapters we will see how these various ideals combine and overlap in gender formation, but for heuristic reasons I have constructed this discussion around local, national and religious discourses. It should also be borne in mind that while there are official discourses of gender ideals, these ideals are interpreted differently by individuals and are played out in daily life in various ways, as this book demonstrates.

IS GENDER IMPORTANT?

Gender Downplayed

Foreign observers of South Sulawesi society might be excused for assuming that gender is not a particularly salient aspect of Bugis social life. Many commentators find evidence for the insignificance of gender in the apparent relative equality of women and men. In the early nineteenth century, Sir Thomas Stamford Raffles (1817: Appendix CLXXIX), the notable British colonial administrator, commented that women in South Sulawesi were held in "more esteem than could be expected from the state of civilisation in general, and undergo none of the severe hardships, privations, or labours that restrict fecundity in other parts of the world." A few years later, the Scottish-born Dr. John Crawfurd (1820: 61–62), who became Resident at the Court of Yogyakarta in Java, noted that among the people of Sulawesi, women in particular "enjoy privileges seldom yielded to them among barbarians." Crawfurd went on to note that women played key roles in business and occasionally became rulers (1820: 74).

Another famous early traveler to the region was Sir James Brooke, the Englishman who became the Rajah of Sarawak in Borneo. He observed that all the offices of state, including even that of Head of the Elders, were open to women and that women actually filled important posts in the government. At the time of Brooke's visit, four of the six great chiefs of the region of **Wajo'** were women. "These ladies," Brooke (1848: 75) wrote, "appear in public like the men; ride, rule, and visit even foreigners, without the knowledge or consent of their husbands."

For more contemporary foreign observers, gender difference may also seem to be downplayed. While his thesis is now refuted, Geertz's (1973a) notion of a "unisex society" has been particularly powerful in encouraging a view of Indonesia as a society where gender is not significantly marked—interestingly, Geertz's notion of a "unisex society", and the idea that sexual differentiation is culturally played down in Bali, only appeared in a footnote (1973a: 417–418, fn. 4), suggesting that gender was not considered a significant topic at the time of his fieldwork. Clothing and accoutrements may also provide evidence of negligible gender difference. For instance, for some people the sarong does not gender the body like dresses or trousers do.

The relative lack of gender-related life-cycle rituals in Indonesia may be another reason why some observers think gender is not clearly articulated in Bugis South Sulawesi. While ceremonial clitoridectomies are performed at places I am familiar with in Bugis South Sulawesi, they are largely symbolic. The prepubescent girl's clitoris is pecked by a hen or a tiny part is snipped with a knife in order to draw blood. Immediately after the procedure, the girl is physically fine to move around. But a Bugis girl's entry into womanhood is certainly not marked by extreme rituals such as tattooing, scarring or foot-binding.

As mentioned in Chapter 1, neither the Bugis nor Indonesian languages have gender-specific singular third-person pronouns, like in English, to distinguish women (she, her) and men (he, his, him). What is linguistically more significant in the Indonesian and Bugis vernacular is relative age. So I do not refer to my host-siblings as my brothers or sisters, but rather, I refer to them by whether they are older or younger than me. So in Indonesian, I use **Kakak** to refer to an older sibling; if I am specifically saying his or her name, I may shorten *Kakak* to *Kak,* for example, *Kak Qadri'*. **Adik** is the term used in Indonesian to refer to a younger sibling. If further clarification is needed, then the sex of the person is added (*adik laki-laki,* "younger brother"). This lack of gender differentiation provides evidence for some people that age, and the status that age confers, is a more important definer of identity than gender in general Indonesian and Bugis society.

The Indonesian media also encourages gender equality, through advertisements for instance. In 2002, an Indonesian television advertisement was screened showing a father telling his daughter that he and her mother were almost the same, except of course for the fact that he had a beard. The daughter laughed, and the father continued by saying that just because women and men are physically different, it does not mean people should treat them differently. The daughter then excitedly asked if this meant she could become a pilot. The father answered that of course she could, as long as she was capable (**mampu**). A male voice-over then announced that while women and men are indeed different, it is not acceptable to discriminate (*perempuan dan lelaki memang beda, tapi tidak berarti boleh dibeda-bedakan*).

There is evidence, then, to suggest that gender in both Bugis and Indonesian societies is a relatively unimportant definer of social identity and that gender plays a limited role in social organization. Is it possible, though, that gender is actually an important concept in Bugis South Sulawesi but that it is just not articulated in ways that people from outside the region instantly recognize? In order to explore this prospect in more depth, I next look at Bugis notions of social status.

Gendered Status

When traveling to a new place, you cannot help but notice things that are strikingly different from what you are used to. One thing that struck me when arriving in South Sulawesi was the importance of social status. Of course, I was not the first to notice this, and there has been much written by both local people and foreigners about the centrality of social status in South Sulawesi society.[2] For the most part, though, these observers have not written about the ways in which gender considerations underpin claims for social status. In order to demonstrate the significance of gender in Bugis society, I want to show how efforts to acquire social status are regulated by gender norms.

There is no doubt that status and issues of social location are important in Bugis society. The centrality of status became clear for me after one particular incident. One evening my host-grandmother, Puang Sari, had a number of women friends over for dinner. Afterward the women sat around gossiping and discussing potential marriage alliances, a favorite topic. At one point Puang Sari, whose social status is incredibly high, began having a coughing attack. I raced to get her a glass of water. I then approached Puang Sari and placed the glass of water on the small table beside her. Although I took the water to her in a crouched position and made sure not to look directly at her, I had neglected to put the glass on a saucer. When I moved away, all the women gasped because it is highly disrespectful to present a glass without its saucer. The other women quickly began fussing, and soon a saucer was brought and Puang Sari gratefully took a drink. For me, this event highlighted the importance of status in Bugis society.

One scholar who has written about the significance of status among Bugis is Susan Millar (1983, 1989). From reading Millar's work, I learned a great deal about status, but I was always left with a niggling question about the relationship between gender and status. Millar (1983: 478) mentions that the Bugis gender system is highly elaborated and formal, but she does not think that gender forms a key organizational principle. Millar (1983: 477) also asserts that the importance of gender is lost in the struggle for status and that gender relations in Bugis society are almost entirely subsidiary to a cultural preoccupation with hierarchical social location.

I do not want to undermine the significance of social status in Bugis South Sulawesi. Rather, I want to examine ways in which gender actually defines appropriate means whereby individuals can attain or lose status. So I do not dispute that status is still the overarching concern, but I posit that the importance of gender is revealed by the fact that gender norms must be followed in order for an individual to earn status. I even want to suggest that ideal models of masculinity and femininity are nowhere more clearly articulated than in struggles for social status—by epitomizing Bugis gender ideals, people improve their social location.

One way in which we can see how gender underpins status is by looking at the types of people who are awarded high social status. Some of the most revered people in Bugis society are those who are bestowed the title of *tau malisé,* a Bugis term that literally means "a person densely filled up" (Millar, 1983: 479). *Tau malisé* have an abundance of desired qualities, such as reason, authority, self-discipline, a degree of refinement or nobleness (**malebbi',** B), physical strength, and aggression. People can increase their chance of becoming *tau malisé* by doing certain things, like getting an education, being economically successful, and traveling far from home and returning wealthy. Indeed, wealth can compensate for a lack of inherited status, and it can thus improve a person's marriage chances. For instance, a wealthy person may be able to marry a person of higher social status in a practice called **mangngelli dara,** which is a Bugis phrase that literally means "to buy blood," but it also means "to buy social status."

Theoretically, both women and men can become *tau malisé.* In reality, though, it is really only men who achieve this title. Instead of becoming *tau malisé* themselves, women are expected to attract the support and protection of a *tau malisé* (Millar, 1983: 491, fn. 6). So for women, gender ideals do not consist of traveling alone far from home, being assertive in public settings, or becoming wealthy. However, if a man does not follow the prescriptions outlined, he may become known as a **tau massissi lalo,** a Bugis title that implies that a person is not considered densely filled up. If a man is labeled a *tau massissi lalo,* his social status goes down.

The importance of status in Bugis society is thus clearly apparent, and in order to gain status and achieve the title of *tau malisé,* individuals must conform to very particular gender ideals. But these gender ideals are masculine ideals and appropriate only for men; women are not encouraged to conform to the prescriptions of being a *tau malisé.* So the ways to achieve social status are highly gendered, and claims for social status require conformity to masculine and feminine ideals. Moreover, when status contestations do occur, they happen between women or between men. For example, men are in constant competition with other men, not with women. These factors suggest the underlying importance of gender in Bugis society.

Another arena to look at if we want to see how gender underpins status considerations is weddings. Weddings are incredibly important events in Bugis society (Idrus, 2003, 2004). Weddings provide the opportunity to catch up with old acquaintances and to form new alliances. A wedding is also an occasion where people get the chance to dress up and impress people with their material wealth. Social status thus becomes a central issue of concern in weddings. But weddings are also places where gender considerations are fundamental. I look more closely at weddings in Chapter 7, so here I just examine how gender considerations underpin status concerns at Bugis weddings.

Bugis marriages should be between a woman and a man of equal social status. Men may marry women of lower social status, but it is uncommon for women to marry men of lower social status. This ban on women marrying down is mentioned in the extensive indigenous document referred to as the **La Galigo** epic cycle. The *La Galigo* epic cycle, which recounts the story of the creation of the Middle World and the first six generations of its inhabitants, is longer in content than the *Mahabharata* and comparable to the adventures of Ulysses in Homer's *Odyssey.* In one of the stories contained within the *La Galigo* cycle, a man by the name of I La Bulisa' marries a woman of higher status. I La Bulisa' is punished for this transgression by supernatural forces, and he eventually dies from bloating of the stomach (Andaya, 2000: 35). The moral of the story is that marrying someone of inappropriate social status will result in catastrophe.

Sir James Brooke (1848: 73–74) also noted the importance of status in Bugis marriage. He wrote, "As no nation grants greater privileges to high birth, so no people are more tenacious of the purity of their descent." Brooke continued by noting, "A woman of pure blood never can marry any but of her own class; but men mix their blood in marriage with the daughters of freemen."

These narratives show that status considerations have long been of primary concern in Bugis marriage negotiations. But these narratives also show that whom an individual is legitimately able to marry is governed by gender concerns; women should not marry men of lower social status than themselves. Status considerations are thus clearly gendered in respect to Bugis marriage.

Rituals surrounding weddings also indicate the importance of achieved and ascribed social status. However, such rituals are underpinned by strict gender considerations. If a woman plans to marry, the set of rules governing the payment of the bride-price must be closely adhered to, although interpretations of these rules are often hotly debated. Usually the bride should receive a higher payment (*sompa,* B) than was paid for her mother. So social status determines who should marry whom, but the proscriptions and rituals surrounding marriage are different for men and for women and are thus gendered.

Seating arrangements at weddings show the importance of both status and gender. Guests are generally not able to choose where they sit at a wedding. Rather, guests are seated according to their relative social status; the higher the person's status, the closer to the front he or she is seated. A person's status is thus publicly shown. But seating arrangements are also highly gendered. Wedding guests are often divided based on gender. For instance, women sit on the left side of the room and men sit on the right side, although the married couple sits side-by-side. While status confusion may occur—for example, a woman of higher status may be wrongly seated behind a woman of lower status—at most weddings women will never sit on the men's side.

Social status is of vital concern in Bugis society, particularly in respect to marriage. However, status contestations are underpinned by strict gender codes. What I now look at is the particular gender ideals promoted within Bugis society.

GENDER IDEALS

What constitute ideal gender types in Bugis society? Who should male-born and female-born individuals aspire to be like? In order to examine Bugis gender more thoroughly, this section discusses gender ideals that are disseminated from three different levels, and it shows how these respective discourses combine in the construction of Bugis gender norms. First, I explore gender ideals as they are promoted from a local Bugis level. In this respect I analyze the honor/shame complex (*siri'*, B). Second, I look at gender norms that arise at the national Indonesian level. Finally, I consider religious narratives and look at what Islamic proscriptions present as desired gender models. Understanding both Bugis gender ideals, which incorporate Indonesian and Islamic norms, and the gendered environment in which gendered identities are created, is important in order to fully appreciate the three alternative gender subjectivities explored in subsequent chapters.

Gendering Shame

In Bugis society, an important regulator of gender behavior is the concept of *siri'*. *Siri'* is a hard word to translate into English. It means "shame," but it also means "a sense of honor." To provide the term with some context, I give the following example: A woman is seen as the primary symbol of her family's *siri'*. If a woman's *siri'* is damaged, this can disgrace her entire family and cause them all to feel *siri'*. So the term *siri'* suggests a complex mix of shame and honor.[3]

Siri' is a useful concept to use when examining Bugis gender ideals. The pervasiveness of *siri'* means that most women adhere to norms of femininity because they do not want to cause their family to feel *siri'*. *Siri'* also acts as a guide to encourage men to embody ideals of masculinity, thus preserving their family's *siri'*. Because a woman is seen as embodying her family's *siri'*, her actions and behaviors are often closely guarded. If a woman causes *siri'*, though, it is not entirely her fault. A woman's brothers share responsibility for protecting their sister and for reacting aggressively in defense of their family's soured reputation. Here we begin to see how ideals of femininity and masculinity are governed by *siri'* considerations.

Siri' has long been a significant concept in South Sulawesi, and it remains so today. The centrality of *siri'* is noted in early Bugis texts, like the *La Galigo* epic cycle, and it has subsequently been written about by local people and travelers to the region. When Hendrik Chabot (1996) was in Sulawesi in the 1940s, he noted that contact between a young, unmarried woman and a man made the woman's male relatives feel *siri'*. These men, Chabot revealed, felt immense shame and anger, and they were subsequently expected to kill the couple or else lose their own honor and self-respect. If the men did not react in an appropriate way, they were considered socially dead (**maté siri'**, B), and they were despised throughout the community (Chabot, 1996: 234–255).

During my fieldwork, I heard of contemporary cases of *siri'* revenge. One case involved a husband who had left his wife and moved in with his mistress. The wife, upon coming across her husband's mistress sitting in a pedicab at the village market, pulled out the small **badi'** knife that she always carried in her sarong and stabbed the mistress to death.

Less dramatically, *siri'* conventions are used in daily life to encourage proper behavior. Mothers beseech their daughters to change into more formal attire if the family is expecting guests. A shabbily dressed daughter would cause her family to feel *siri'*. Fathers command their sons not to cry in public, so people will not consider the boy to be cowardly, which would cause the boy's family to feel *siri'*.

Siri' issues affect whole families, so strict measures are in place to make sure that *siri'* offenses never occur. Women are particularly well-guarded so that they do not cause feelings of *siri'* to arise. A woman's position is a fixed point against which her close male relatives measure their social status. If an unmarried woman becomes pregnant, for instance, the social status of her brothers and her entire family suffers. As a result of a *siri'* violation like this, the woman's brothers may find it hard to secure a good marriage. If an unmarried man becomes a father, it is likely that his family will suffer less severe status repercussions than if he were an unmarried pregnant woman. So if a woman loses social standing by causing *siri'*, the repercussions for all concerned are particularly calamitous.

The ramifications of a woman causing *siri'* are so great that women's activities are particularly regulated and often subject to vigilant surveillance. Puang Sulai, a conservative Bugis man, told me that women are more nurtured and protected than men precisely because if women cause *siri'*, the results for their entire family are disastrous. To guard against this possibility, it is considered essential that women receive careful nurturing so that they know what constitutes appropriate feminine behavior and so that they are fully aware of the imperative to conform to gender ideals.

One way in which ideal femininity is achieved is through ensuring that women do not travel alone over great distances or after dark. If a woman travels on her own, she is considered to be at risk of inviting a *siri'* violation. A single woman is vulnerable to the advances of a man, for instance. For this reason, if a woman travels, even around her home town, she should preferably have a companion (**pendamping**). Females who do travel alone may be viewed with suspicion, and if they travel alone too often they may no longer be considered good women; although of course in reality Bugis women go overseas to study and travel, often on their own. In Chapter 2, I introduced Maman, Rani, and Dilah and revealed how these females travel alone in clear acts of defiance against ideals of femininity. Traveling alone helps ensure that Maman, Rani, and Dilah are not considered good women, and this is precisely what they want. Traveling alone can help females confirm their status as calalai.

As a foreign woman, my position in Bugis society was particularly interesting. I was considered a woman, but in order to be considered an ideal woman in a Bugis context, I would not have been able to travel alone. Such a restraint would have made fieldwork difficult, and it would have also felt very restrictive to have someone monitor my every movement. Whenever I mentioned I was going for a walk during the day, various members of the household would volunteer, or volunteer someone else, to accompany me. Sometimes I just wanted to be on my own, which my host-family found an odd proposition as solitude is not something that tends to be valued, so I would politely but adamantly refuse the offer. I did follow many proscriptions about travel, though. For instance, when I was staying in Sengkang, I always made sure I was home before the evening prayers (*magrib*), which start around 6 p.m., and I never went anywhere on my own after dark. But I did of course travel between towns on my own, and many people thought this was far too brave (*terlalu berani*) an action for a woman. While the word *berani* has positive connotations for a man, when it is applied to a woman it means she is being too headstrong and assertive, not qualities an ideal woman should possess.

When I was out on my own, I was frequently greeted with puzzled faces and questions of concern about my safety. But I never felt unsafe as there were always people who took me under their wing. For example, one day I was in a minivan (*pētē-pētē*) and someone saw the nametag on my backpack and read the word *Australia*. It was during the East Timor crisis, and Australia—and by association, Australians—was not considered in a particularly good light, especially as the United States had just nominated Australia to be its "Deputy Sheriff" in the region. The man started verbally abusing me because he saw Australia as stealing East Timor away from Indonesia. The man's diatribe made me feel quite nervous. Thankfully, the woman next to me leaned toward the man and stated firmly, "Leave her alone. It is not her fault what her country is doing." When I related this story to my host-family later that night, instead of praising the woman who had stood up for me, the incident reaffirmed for them that I should not travel alone.

But my host-family and others accepted that I was going to keep traveling on my own because, even though I was a woman, I was a foreign woman, and as such I was an intriguing anomaly—at 24, I was neither married nor divorced, I had no children, and my parents had allowed me to come to a distant country on my own. My identity was incongruous, so my indiscretions were largely dismissed as aberrations.

There were definitely advantages to being a foreign woman in terms of accessing gendered spaces. I was a woman, so I was allowed to enter female spaces like kitchens and bedrooms, and I was a foreigner, which gave me quasi-men's status, meaning that I was often expected to eat first with the men and afterwards to sit at the front of the house and engage in conversation with them. These experiences and open access to particular places gave me further insights into concepts of gender and how *siri'* considerations define gender ideals.

Prescriptions of masculinity, like femininity, are also clearly defined in Bugis society, although such ideals are not necessarily adhered to by all people at all times, and people often interpret these ideals differently. If a man does not behave appropriately in a *siri'* situation, he is considered to have ceased all meaningful involvement in the world. Chabot (1996: 237), writing of neighboring Makassar, records the story of a man who stabbed his sister after an accidental encounter with her on the street. While the man showed no remorse for his deed, he was sad that he had bumped into his sister and that she was now dead. But the man felt that if he was to be regarded as an honorable man, he had no other option but to kill his sister. The man could not just kill his sister any way he chose, though; the honorable way of killing in *siri'* instances is by stabbing the person with a *badi'* knife in the open. If a man does what is socially expected of him according to norms of masculinity, he confirms his status as a man, and he reaffirms both his and his family's social location. So we can see how gender behavior is governed at the local level by *siri'* considerations: Women must avoid causing shame by acting appropriately (e.g., marrying a suitably ranked man), and men must properly avenge any attacks on their family's honor. Of course, though, these are ideals, and not everyone conforms to these models all of the time.

With such strong gender ideals, it is essential that children are instructed about appropriate gender behavior. Girls are taught early on about the importance of marriage. Marriage is particularly significant for women because it allows them to legitimately have children, and this is how they achieve the revered Bugis status of **Indo'** (Mother). During fieldwork, I would often watch my two host-nieces playing. In their play they would, like most girls, copy the roles they are expected to assume when they grow up. One time, I was reading Chang Jung's (1991) novel, *Wild Swans*. On the cover is a picture of the author, her mother, and her grandmother. When I put the book down, my 7-year-old host-niece excitedly picked it up. Lilah nursed the book in her arms and, using an Eveready battery, fed Jung "milk" through the battery "bottle." Lilah was copying the nurturing role she will ideally take on when she becomes a mother. Lilah used great improvisation in her play, too; she did not own a doll, but she easily substituted a book for her play toy.

On another occasion, I was reading Herdt's (1994) anthology *Third Sex/Third Gender*. My twin 4-year-old host-nephews were chasing each other through my legs. One of them soon caught sight of the book. He grabbed it and inspected the cover closely before pronouncing **Ibu** (Mother) and *Bapak* (Father), pointing to the respective individuals. The actual anatomical sex of the individuals was unclear from the cover photo, but my host-nephew had learned the visible signs of masculinity and femininity (e.g., men have short hair, women wear make-up). Comprehending the visual representations of women and men is something that children grasp from a young age.

Courting and associated behavior are also regulated by *siri'* considerations, and these considerations are in turn highly gendered. At adolescence, sexuality becomes an issue of central importance, and gender ideals and norms become particular burdens for individuals to a degree not previously known. Modesty, protection, and proper behavior become matters of concern. Girls must now dress modestly, and cowardly behavior is unacceptable for boys. Moreover, girls and boys are no longer able to play freely together.

The social settings where unmarried people can associate in contemporary Bugis society are still somewhat guarded, particularly in rural areas. Festivals and weddings, therefore, become key places for young adults to meet. I described in Chapter 2 a Bugis festival I attended with Khadija. The reason that Khadija was so keen to go to this festival was because it was an opportunity for her to legitimately associate with boys—she referred to this as an opportunity to *cuci mata* (literally, "wash her eyes"). Some of my other friends went to great lengths to get invited to as many weddings as possible. My friends knew that weddings were appropriate social settings to meet eligible bachelors.

In urban areas, regulating teenage behavior is somewhat more challenging, and youths find ways to meet prospective partners at places such as cinemas, sporting events, school, public spaces such as shopping malls, and through family acquaintances (e.g., an older brother may bring friends home to visit). Many couples nowadays find that they are able to at least form friendships before marriage, as we will see in Chapter 7. However, intimate time alone may not be legitimately possible for a young couple. Of course on a practical level, many couples do establish intimate relationships before marriage (Bennett, 2005). Indeed, two of my close Bugis friends lived together at the boyfriend's parental home for five years before they got married in 2004.

Individuals, particularly women, are under a great deal of pressure to marry, and few females are prepared to jeopardize their family's *siri'* by not marrying heterosexually. There are a few notable exceptions of Bugis women remaining unmarried. Indeed, my host-grandmother was of such high status that there was no man of higher rank for her to marry. In general, though, if a woman remains unmarried and without children, her family's *siri'* is threatened (Idrus, 2003). As we will see in Chapter 4, because calalai remain unmarried in a legal sense, they potentially cause their families to feel great *siri'*. Calalai challenge gender norms in other ways too, and such behaviors serve to reinforce what females should not do if they want to be considered ideal women. Calalai are seen as assertive, a trait not suitable for women. The assertive, and sometimes aggressive behavior of calalai may also result in their families feeling *siri'*.

The repercussions of ignoring ideals of gender make it surprising that anyone does ignore gender ideals to any great degree. Indeed, in some places so few females radically ignore gender ideals that people have not heard of calalai, **lesbi**, or **hunter**. I remember asking a man named Pak Gaob why there were so many calabai in Sengkang but not many calalai. He was not actually sure whom I was referring to and asked me if by calalai I meant people with female genitalia but who are inclined to be men (*maksudnya, jenis kelaminan wanita, cenderung lelaki*). When I said yes, he responded that he did not know why there were not many calalai in Sengkang, and he said in fact he had never met a calalai. It is possible that Pak Gaob politely did not notice or acknowledge calalai in order to avoid the *siri'* it might cause that person's family. But throughout my fieldwork, I found that people who knew of calalai were generally forthcoming with information, and while theoretically having a calalai relative may cause *siri'*, in practice this was certainly not always the case, as we will see in Chapter 4.

Calabai may also cause their family to feel *siri'*. However, the different values placed on females and males means that feelings of *siri'* are less likely to occur as the result of a son identifying as calabai than of a daughter identifying as calalai. It is not so much being calabai per se that potentially causes *siri'* but a calabai's failure to avenge family honor—I talk about this issue more in Chapter 5. The consequences of a man or a calabai not defending the family's honor, or of a woman or a calalai not becoming a wife and mother, can unsettle an entire family. There is no respected role model for individuals to assume other than the official model regulated through *siri'*. If an individual does not conform to normative gender models (masculine-male man, feminine-female woman), he or she is left without a legitimate model of personhood. If an individual is female and masculine, s/he may be labeled calalai because there is no legitimate model of being a masculine woman; similarly, feminine males may be labeled calabai—as we will see in later chapters, female masculinity and male femininity do not necessarily conform to ideals of masculinity and feminity.

People in South Sulawesi, like people everywhere, are socialized through powerful norms that prescibe what being born female or being born male should mean. Michel Foucault (1977) has written about this, and he argues that people internalize gender ideals and because people then habitually conform to these ideas, they become ideal citizens. While *siri'* has changed over time—for instance, men and single women can now make eye contact without causing *siri'*—*siri'* continues to regulate gender norms. In a way, it is because *siri'* is dynamic that it has managed to stay relevant to today's society.

So far we have looked at how local factors contribute to Bugis gender ideals. The Indonesian government also presents a view of ideal gender types. It is essential to examine these ideals when exploring Bugis gender because the formation of a gendered self in South Sulawesi develops in reference to these wider concerns. I turn now to national government gender discourses to see how these define gender ideals.

Government Gender Discourses

In a variety of ways, the Indonesian government disseminates the gender ideals to which it thinks its citizens should adhere. The government sends out gender messages through the mass media, educational avenues such as school curricula (Parker, 1992, 2002), and through social services such as health care clinics and development agencies. So what do these discourses promote as ideal gender types? While here I am interested primarily in what is promoted at official levels, in later chapters I will explore how individuals interpret these discourses.

The national government clearly states what Indonesian men should ideally be like. Men should marry heterosexually and, once married, they should assume the role of primary income earner, thus providing their wives and children with financial support. As head of the household, men should make decisions in the best interest of their family. In many contexts, only men can validly interact in the social arena and publicly represent their family's interests. To an extent, a man's masculinity is measured by the purity and morality of his family—we see here the overlapping relationship between national gender ideologies and Bugis notions of *siri'*. So it is a man's responsibility to protect his family. Essential qualities for men to possess, and which men need in order to undertake their assigned roles, include reason, rationality, self-discipline, and control of their emotions and passions. It is these qualities that make men worthy of being head of the household and the primary wage earner. Moreover, possession of these qualities differentiates men from women. Islam, as we will see shortly, reinforces these notions of ideal masculinity.

Men in Indonesia should assume active roles that generally take place outside of the home. Physical strength is a desired masculine quality needed for roles such as cutting down coconuts (Figure 3.1) and plowing rice fields (Figure 3.2). Men are also considered more ideally suited to roles that involve travel and transport, such as delivering produce to markets (Figure 3.3).

Indonesian government discourses also clearly describe ideals of womanhood. In many ways, women are defined in opposition to men. For instance, women are assumed not to possess the quality of reason in as much abundance as men. Rather, women are thought to be passionate and emotional, and they are considered to be guided by these factors. As such, women are often deemed ineffective family heads, although in practice women serve as effective household heads. Women are regarded as less controlled and restrained than men, and they are also judged more likely to be materialistic and gossipy (Brenner, 1996).

Girls are taught from a young age that their greatest accomplishments will be becoming a wife and mother. Indeed, these accomplishments are often considered to be women's natural roles. When a woman marries and bears children, she can become a legitimate citizen and a full member of the Indonesian nation-state. If a woman does not marry and have children, she will not automatically be granted full citizenship (Blackwood, 1995). Within their roles as wife and mother, women are expected to be primarily responsible for the upkeep of their household and for ensuring that their house is clean and that their family is well fed (Figures 3.4, 3.5).

While ideals of womanhood have long existed in Indonesia, it was during President Suharto's New Order period (1965–1998)—so named to make it sound progressive and modern and to separate it from the preceding Guided Democracy period of President Sukarno's reign (1945–1965)—that womanhood became strictly defined and women's roles became almost entirely centered within the home. The nuclear family was promoted as the ideal family type, and the slogan "Two Kids Are Enough" (*Dua Anak Cukup*) appeared ad nauseum. The duties of women were structured to show their decreasing importance. First and foremost, a woman must marry heterosexually. Only once married can a woman legitimately have children and become a full member of society. If a woman does not conform to these ideals, she may not be

FIGURE 3.1 A man collecting coconuts

FIGURE 3.2 Men working in the rice fields

FIGURE 3.3 A man delivering produce

FIGURE 3.4 A woman preparing a meal

FIGURE 3.5 A woman cooking coconut milk to make coconut oil

considered a perfect woman (*perempuan yang sempurna*) or a complete woman (*perempuan yang lengkap*).

The Indonesian government has further ways of promoting the adoption of ideal gender roles. The government requires heterosexual marriage from its civil servants. As the government believes that civil servants represent the state and thus act as a symbol of the morality of the nation and the level of control the government has over its citizenry, civil servants are expected to set a good example for the rest of society. Furthermore, female homosexuality has been considered a contravention of women's natural destiny to become mothers and is not in accordance with Indonesian culture (Gayatri, 1995). Indonesian women have made impressive gains in such fields as politics, but even during her reign, former President Megawati Sukarnoputri noted that her domestic duties were not neglected as a result of her public commitments. The Indonesian government thus promotes ideal gender roles in a variety of ways, and many of these ideals operate in a mutually reinforcing relationship with Bugis notions of *siri'* and, as we will now see, Islam.

Islam and Gender

Throughout the thirteenth, fourteenth, and fifteenth centuries, the influence of Islam grew steadily in Indonesia. Trade was an essential element in bringing Islam to the archipelago, although the conversion of members of the nobility, influenced by visiting learned Muslim clerics, had the most profound impact in terms of local adoption of this religion (Ricklefs, 1993). While Islam spread throughout South Sulawesi much later than in other Indonesian regions, such as Sumatra and Java, when the ruler of the South Sulawesi kingdom of Goa converted to Islam early in the seventeenth century, local people and rulers adopted Islam with incredible speed. The fast pace at which Islam then took hold in South Sulawesi was due in no small part to the fact that the new ruler of Goa believed it his religious duty to bring this new faith to his neighbors, by conquest if necessary (Andaya, 1981). Today, over 95 percent of Bugis, the largest ethnic group in South Sulawesi, adhere to Islam, although as we will see, especially in Chapter 6, pre-Islamic and syncretic beliefs and rituals are still evident. Islam thus shapes Bugis gender ideals to a great extent.

In the nineteenth century, James Brooke (1848: 89–90) noted that women in South Sulawesi "enjoy perfect liberty, and are free from all the restraints usually imposed by the Mohammedan religion." Indeed, Muslim women throughout Indonesia have historically enjoyed a high social status relative to Muslim women living in regions such as the Middle East. For instance, Muslim women in Indonesia in general have considerable economic independence in terms of earning and spending their own income, and they tend to enjoy spatial mobility in the public sphere (Bennett, 2002; Brenner, 1998; Sullivan, 1994). Girls, just like boys, receive primary and secondary schooling, and there is not a clear preference for sons over daughters. Indonesian Muslim women are not required to completely cover their bodies, and the wearing of headdress tends to be an individual choice (Brenner, 1996). Nevertheless, Islam does promote clear gender ideals for Indonesian Muslim women. For instance, to be good Muslims, women should be heterosexual wives and devoted mothers. Only by fulfilling these roles do Indonesian women become full Muslim citizens.

Muslim men in Indonesia are also governed by gender ideals. Within Islam, men are equated with being husbands, workers, and responsible members of society. Ideal Muslim masculinity is often related to the notion of chivalry, not seeing oneself as superior to others, not having enemies, acting justly, and having a good character. Being noble, loyal, generous, and courageous and sacrificing oneself for family and friends are all espoused as desirable Muslim masculine qualities. Male-born Muslims in Indonesia are considered to be complete men when they marry heterosexually, father children, become the head of their household, provide income and food for their family, and are able to represent their family in the public arena (Idrus, 2004).

Islam promotes specific ideals for Indonesian Muslim women and men in terms of sexuality. The ideal of premarital chastity holds true for both women and for men, but female virginity is more highly valued. The regulation of female sexuality before marriage is reinforced by other discourses in Indonesia too, such as government discourses and notions of siri', as we have seen in previous sections.

Marriage is assigned tremendous importance in Islam—indeed, gender ideals are often synonymous with qualities expected of wives and husbands. Islam states that all Muslims are morally required to marry heterosexually, and it is only when married that women and men can legitimately become parents and full members of society. One particular saying goes that when a man marries, he has completed half of his religion, and he needs only to fear Allah to complete the other half. The emphasis that every Muslim should be married if possible reflects the notion that the ideal relationship between a man and a woman can only occur within marriage. Within Indonesian Islam, there is no popular model of same-sex couples, of unmarried couples, or of parents who are not married.

Islam in Indonesia promotes particular standards of public behavior and dress for women and men. Islam may be used to regulate women's social conduct and it may also be used to confine women's movements. For instance, the Qur'an, the Islamic holy book, may be cited as the basis for restricting women from going out at night; indeed *ma'grib* prayers often serve as an indictor for when women should be home. Islam may also be used to define Indonesian Muslim women in opposition to the perceived Western capitalistic and individualistic woman. In terms of dress and demeanor, Muslim women in Indonesia are expected to be modest, although Mernissi (1991) and Ahmed (1992) argue that the Qur'an does not explicitly demand that women wear headdress. Similarly, Indonesian Muslim men are guided by the Qur'an in terms of appropriate behavior and dress. For instance, Muslim men should wear conservative clothing that covers most of their body, and they may choose to cover their heads in public. Indonesian Muslim men should also act in a responsible and controlled manner.

Because at the level of discourse gender ideals are so starkly defined in Indonesian and Bugis society, individuals who transgress gender borders are clearly visible. These individuals often become marginal citizens. At the local, national, and religious levels, there are no legitimate examples for people to follow other than the binary heterosexual models of female-feminine woman and masculine-male man. There are, though, many people who do not, or cannot, conform to such strict gender ideals, and we turn to these subjectivities in the following four chapters.

CONCLUSION

This chapter has shown the importance of gender in Bugis South Sulawesi, and it has explored gender ideals presented to Bugis people. In doing so, the chapter was divided into two main sections. The first section looked at whether gender is an important issue in Bugis South Sulawesi. There is a relative dearth of material on gender, especially gender variance, in South Sulawesi, and the few available sources tend to downplay the importance of gender in Bugis society. I used notions of status acquisition and social location to demonstrate that gender is a significant concept in Bugis society. I suggested that while struggles for social location are of vital concern in Bugis life, they are underpinned by gender considerations. Indeed, in order to achieve increased social status, individuals must adhere to strict gender conventions.

In the second part, I began an examination of gender ideals that are presented to people in Bugis South Sulawesi. I initially used the Bugis concept of *siri'* to demonstrate ways in which local norms serve to instruct individuals in the correct way of behaving. Women are considered the primary bearers of family honor, but if honor is damaged, it is the responsibility of male relatives to restore it. Ideal Bugis femininity, then, is defined around notions of avoiding causing *siri'*. Ideal masculinity, on the other hand, is defined around protecting and avenging challenges to a family's *siri'*. I then analyzed normative paradigms of femininity and masculinity as they are shaped through national government ideology and Islamic discourse. I suggested that by emphasizing the roles of women as wives and mothers and the roles of men as the head of the household and the family's public representative, Islam and the government play an instructive role in sculpting Bugis gender ideals.

This chapter serves as a reference point for later discussions on behaviors and identities that do not conform to normative Bugis gender ideals. It is only by knowing the discursive context in which calalai, calabai, and bissu live that their identities can be appreciated and we can achieve a better awareness of the negotiations individuals undertake in developing a gender identity.

ENDNOTES

1. There is a small but growing body of published literature concerning gender in South Sulawesi: Andaya, 2000; Chabot, 1996; Errington, 1989; Graham, 2001, 2003, 2004a, 2004b, 2004c; Hamonic, 1975, 1977a; Idrus, 2003, 2004; Idrus & Bennett, 2003; Kennedy, 1993; Matthes, 1872; Millar, 1983, 1989; Pelras, 1996; Robinson & Paeni, 1998; Rottger-Rossler, 2000; Silvey, 2000a, 2000b; and van der Kroef, 1956.

2. Sources that touch on status in South Sulawesi include the following: Acciaioli, 1989; Andaya, 1981; Caldwell, 1988; Chabot, 1996; Cummings, 2002; Harvey, 1978; Idrus, 2003, 2004; Millar, 1989; Pelras, 1996; Robinson & Paeni, 1998; Rossler, 2000; and Tol, van Dijk, & Acciaioli, 2000.

3. There are some sources published on *siri'* in South Sulawesi. See Chabot, 1996; Errington, 1989; Idrus, 2003; and Millar, 1989.

4

Female Transgendering

A CREM-BATH: A PRELUDE

There are days when I know I should go out and talk with people and see what is happening—after all, it might be the day that some great event happens and I would miss it. But some days I just cannot muster the energy to be friendly, attentive, and inquisitive. Today was one of those days. I would have preferred to stay in my room reading. But alas, I would have felt guilty all day. So I tried to find some activity that would motivate me to get outside. One option was going to Eka's to get a back massage—s/he would have chatted quietly away about interesting gender-related matters while s/he pummeled my back, and I would have been under no obligation, or in any disposition, to respond. But I am in Makassar, and Sengkang is 100 kilometers away, a five-hour car journey. I could have gone down to the foreshore—just sitting there invariably results in people coming up and talking to me. When I told them I was researching gender, if I was lucky, they would have launched into a monologue and I could have just sat taking notes. I could have traveled out to the university and read some more of the literature on Bugis customs—I can always use more information about historical gender ideals. But even that seemed far too taxing. So the option I settled on was going to visit Dilah.

Dilah is working at the moment in a hair-dressing salon, and the salon happens to specialize in crem-bath—*the thought of a relaxing* crem-bath *definitely sparked my interest. When Dilah first mentioned that I should come to the salon for a* crem-bath, *I had visions of a bathtub full of some kind of milky lotion. But, as often is the case, my presumption was entirely wrong. A* crem-bath *is a moisturizing hair treatment, and it includes a delicious head massage. I arrived at the salon around 11 a.m.—one need not start field-work too early on days like this—and Dilah was there, along with Eri and Ella. The salon is the perfect place for casual chats about all things to do with gender.*

Today's topic of conversation started quite generally but soon moved on to gender acquisition. Dilah is one of nine daughters, and because hir parents really wanted a son, they kind of chose hir to be the boy. S/he thinks this is a major reason why s/he is so masculine now.

 *It is weird how at the end of the day my friends become informants. Writing here makes today seem somehow different to when I was hanging out. When I sit down to write notes, even casual conversations become analytic insights into another way of life. I was reading over some of my early field notes before and had to chuckle when I read, "I must report to the **Bupati**'s (Regent's) office tomorrow to get him to sign all the official research papers. If he signs them, then I can officially start fieldwork tomorrow—but what the %#$! does fieldwork actually involve?" But I guess it is largely this—chatting, observing, and writing about it. But I digress. . . .*

 *After Dilah finished speaking, Eri spoke of a different reason for becoming a masculine female, a calalai. S/he was seduced by a **lines,** a woman attracted to calalai. Becoming involved in a relationship with a lines is what Eri believes caused hir to adopt a calalai gender.*

 *Ella also works at the salon. Ella identifies as calabai, a male-born individual who is more like a woman than a man. Ella prefers the term **waria,** though, to describe hir gender. Waria is a national Indonesian term, and it is a neologism made from **wanita** (woman) and **pria** (man). Ella does not dress as a woman, though, because s/he says s/he gets hassled too much, for instance if s/he dresses as a woman, people whistle at hir when s/he crosses the road. But Ella does feel upset that if s/he wears men's clothes, no one can tell hir inner nature (sifat); people just assume s/he is a man, which s/he is not; s/he is waria. So the salon is a great place to go to talk about all things to do with gender, and today it was especially rewarding because I had a crem-bath!* (Field notes, 2000)

In this excerpt from my field notes, we see some of the reasons why individuals assume a gender identity that is contrary to what society expects; Chapter 2 explored such reasons in more depth. There are clear gender models that individuals in Bugis South Sulawesi are encouraged to conform to, and there is a lot of pressure for individuals, especially females, to do this, as Chapter 3 showed. But not everyone finds it natural or easy to assume the gender ideals society expects of them. In some societies, gender definitions are rather broad, and it is difficult for a female to be seen as anything other than a woman. Living in the United States, Australia, or New Zealand, I can be extremely masculine; dress, act, and behave like a man; and be involved in a romantic relationship with a woman. By doing these things, though, I would not exclude myself from the category of "woman." I might be called "butch" or a tomboy because of a masculine identity, or a lesbian in relation to sexuality, but I would still be considered a woman. From my experience in South Sulawesi, the definition of a woman is very strict, and female-born individuals who do not act like women may be seen as other than women.

 There are a few terms used to describe masculine females with same-sex sexual desires in Bugis South Sulawesi. Dilah uses the term *hunter* to describe hir identity. For hir, this English-derived term implies an assertive identity, describing someone who actively pursues goals and dreams. Other people prefer to use the term ***tomboi.*** For them, *tomboi,* also derived from English, connotes masculine behavior. Some people use *lesbi,* from the English *lesbian,* to describe masculine females who form intimate relationships with other females, although many people see the term *lesbi* as erroneously overemphasizing sexuality. The term *calalai* is also used in Bugis South Sulawesi. While *calalai*[1] is a Bugis term, literally meaning "false man," calalai identity is developed in reference to national and international ideas disseminated via the mass media and through individuals traveling and bringing certain thoughts and trends home. There is no single calalai identity, and some individuals do not associate themselves with this term at all. However, I have selected to use the term *calalai* in this book in preference to other terms in order to situate this ethnography within Bugis South Sulawesi, although when quoting informants I retain the term they use. I also use the term *lines,* which is used in some areas to refer to the feminine partners of calalai.

A CLOISTERED IDENTITY

I was in Sulawesi many months before I met anyone who identified as calalai. For a while, I was starting to think that perhaps no one did identify as such anymore. In conversations with people about gender, I would often ask about calalai. On many occasions, people would not know whom I was referring to, so I would need to describe calalai identity, saying calalai are female-born individuals who are more like men than women in their dress, behavior, and roles. Sometimes people were familiar with such an identity after I explained it, although often their accounts were quite superficial, sometimes drawing on their knowledge of the past to present information about anomalous females. I have used the word *cloistered,* which means "reclusive," "secluded," or "sequestered," in the title to this section to represent that calalai identity tends to remain in the background of Bugis society.

When I asked Puang Bachri, a well-respected Bugis man, if he knew of any calalai, he recounted a number of historical tales. Puang Bachri said the last Raja of Balannipa, a town near Majene in Sulawesi, was a calalai. This Raja wielded a great deal of power, Puang Bachri said, and as a sign of hir power s/he had three wives. S/he was a pure-blood Raja, which meant that hir blood was 100 percent white (**darah putih**)—this analogy is akin to the English notion of the aristocracy having blue blood. The Raja was very brave, and s/he wore a man's sarong and carried a pistol. S/he loved hunting and was better than all the men at killing wild game. In addition to hir wives, the Raja also had many beautiful girlfriends, and Puang Bachri said no one minded.

Puang Bachri also told me about a particularly famous calalai who became very, very rich. S/he worked for members of the nobility as a clerk (**punggawa**), and s/he also had hundreds of apprentices (**anak buah**). Puang Bachri said s/he was so strong (**kuat**) and rough (**kasar**) that everyone was afraid of hir.

One day I was talking with Andi Lutfi, a 28-year-old man who comes from a relatively well-off family. The title of *Andi* before his name signifies his high status. Andi Lutfi was one of the first people I met who talked of calalai. When I asked him if he knew anyone who identified as calalai, he replied that he knew a calalai who went by the name of Kak Sul—*Kak* is short for *Kakak,* which means "elder sibling." Kak Sul was 41 years old, he said, and s/he had been living in a de facto relationship, "like husband and wife," with a woman for the last five years. Kak Sul's appearance and behavior are just like a man, Andi Lutfi stated. S/he has short hair, s/he smokes cigarettes, and s/he dresses like a man. Andi Lutfi said that Kak Sul has worked for former President Suharto and a mayor in Jakarta, and they both respectfully preference hir name with *Kak* because they are afraid of offending hir. Kak Sul often goes to people's houses, where s/he tells them about their health and predicts their future. Andi Lutfi said that Kak Sul has supernatural powers; indeed, he referred to hir as a *paranormal*. Andi Lutfi suggested that the high status of Kak Sul stems from hir ability to contact the world of the supernatural. As we will see in Chapter 6, there is a particular effort by some people to associate the power and potency of bissu shamans with sexual ambiguity.

While Andi Lutfi knew a calalai, most people I spoke with were even less familiar than he was with this gender identity. As I noted in Chapter 6, when I asked Pak Gaob, a 30-year-old man, why there were so few calalai in South Sulawesi, he asked me for clarification of what that identity implied. The lack of local awareness of calalai is certainly in stark contrast to popular knowledge about calabai, as we will see in Chapter 5.

Some people offered opinions as to why there are so few calalai, and these opinions reinforced my thinking that strict gender codes operate in Bugis society, particularly in respect to women. Pak Mansur, a 39-year-old man, told me that the reason why there are so few calalai is that women are more guarded by their families than men are. In other words, female-born individuals have much more pressure placed on them to be proper women than male-born individuals do to be proper men. A young man, Yayu, told me that *lesbi,* the word he used for calalai, are less moral than other people and that calalai behavior, especially same-sex sexual behavior, was *tabu* (taboo). As a result, people do not accept calalai, he said. The use of the term *lesbi* by Yayu has negative connotations, and it is a word seen by many calalai as wrongly associating their identity purely with sexual activity.

Another man I spoke with about calalai—interestingly, hardly any women offered opinions on why there are so few calalai visible in society—was Puang Sulai, an elderly high-ranking nobleman. Puang Sulai told me there are not many calalai because they do not have a specific social function. He noted that unlike bissu, who have long-held positions in places such as the royal courts, calalai have never had a particular role in Bugis society. As a result of this, Puang Sulai claims that calalai have a low status in society and as such, it is hard for calalai to be accepted.

Haji Muhammad, a middle-aged religious leader who had recently been on the **hajj** to Mecca, told me that not many calalai can do the work of men, so it is harder for calalai to get the jobs they want. Even where calalai do get appropriate work, it is rarely in public view. For instance, Haji Muhammad said that calalai work in the rice fields and are thus invisible to the rest of society, unlike calabai, who are very noticeable in their work at weddings and in beauty salons. A university student in his mid-20s, named Guf, also picked up on this theme. Guf said there are few calalai because calalai do not have any real role in Bugis society. When I asked Guf why calalai do not create a role for themselves, he replied that would be impossible, as calalai would be competing with men, and Guf did not think that men would give calalai much chance to get a position in society. It is hard for calalai to take on social roles, Guf said, and even where they do, they are competing with men who have more power within the community.

Very few individuals identify themselves publicly as calalai, and there are powerful reasons why they do not. Notions of ideal womanhood are pervasive and exceptionally hard to ignore. If females do not conform to these ideals, it is hard for them to create a unique and productive role. In many ways, the most available model for calalai to conform to is the model of masculinity, and in some respects, following this model grants calalai a level of social acceptance. In establishing a gender identity, then, calalai take on many ideals of masculinity.

CALALAI GENDER

Dilah

Partway into my fieldwork, when I was staying in the city of Makassar visiting a friend, I heard about a beauty pageant that the Australian foreign aid agency (AusAID) was sponsoring. The contestants were all calabai, and the purpose of the event was to bring awareness to issues of HIV/AIDS. I did not particularly feel like going out that night, but I knew it would be exciting and that I was bound to meet a lot of interesting people. My friend, Idam, offered to come with me. We got on his motorbike and, with me securing my oversized helmet with one hand and hanging on to Idam with the other, off we puttered.

The beauty pageant was being held in a big hall in the middle of the city. We paid our Rp10,000 (US$1) entry fee and walked through to the main stage. There were other foreigners (**bule**) there, which was notable because it had been quite a while since I had seen any foreigners—while there was certainly an English-speaking expatriate community in Makassar, I did not network with them. We took seats toward the front of the hall. Walking around the room were stunningly made-up calabai, wearing the most gorgeous dresses. The people I particularly noticed, though, were three feminine-looking men standing in the opposite corner. Idam whispered that they were *hunter*. For the rest of the pageant, all I could think about was how much I would like to hear their views on gender. But how could I meet them? I did not want to simply walk up and say, "Hi, I am studying gender and my friend said you are *hunter*, so I was wondering if I could get your perspective on gender?" It seemed a very impersonal approach and one that I was not comfortable with. But I reconciled with myself that if I did not approach the group now, I might not have the chance again.

At first, it was terribly awkward. Dilah asked me if I was a journalist coming to get a sexy story on the bizarre sex rituals of the exotic Other. I told hir I was not a journalist but that I was a PhD student from Australia, and I was studying Bugis ideas of gender. When they found out I was not a journalist, they seemed to relax a bit, and Dilah started telling me about how society in general reacts to calalai and how it is often very hard for them to get social acceptance. I told hir I was really interested in hir story and that I would love to come and interview hir one day. S/he gave me hir phone number.

Over the next seven months, Dilah and I hung out quite a bit, and through hir I came to have a better understanding of how individuals negotiate nonnormative gender identities. Dilah identifies as Muslim, Bugis, and Indonesian. These allegiances mean that s/he is under a lot of pressure to conform to certain expectations of femininity. There are also forces closer to home that are placing pressure on Dilah to become recognized as a legitimate citizen by marrying a man and having children.

Dilah was in hir late 20s when I first met hir. Although I was a few years younger, in many ways we shared similar predicaments. For instance, there was increasing pressure on both of us to marry and to have children. The pressure was of course received differently; I was keen to both marry heterosexually and have children, and there were many role models available to me of women who did not get married or have children. Dilah's parents, though, were becoming increasingly concerned that their daughter would never marry and bear them grandchildren. Indeed, Dilah's parents became quite proactive on this front and arranged hir marriage a number of times, although Dilah always refused the match. We see then that even though Dilah presents a masculine self, the fact that s/he is female is never forgotten, and the responsibilities that many Bugis see as part and parcel of being female, such as bearing children, are never ignored.

Dilah is not oblivious to these expectations, and s/he is not entirely adverse to all of them. S/he told me that s/he would actually like to have children but that s/he really does not want to get married to a man, a prospect s/he finds repulsive. Dilah once commented that s/he might adopt a baby so that s/he does not have to have sex with a man, but s/he knows that there would be great pressure placed on hir to ensure that hir baby grows up with a father.

In Indonesia it is really only though heterosexual marriage that a female can become a legitimate mother. Dilah recognizes this, and s/he does sometimes mention that s/he would be prepared to marry temporarily in order to have a legitimate child. This compromise on Dilah's part reveals the way in which familial pressure, along with state ideology and Islam, combine in their efforts to shape a person's life. But Dilah does not simply accept these social expectations. Rather, s/he negotiates hir way around gender prescriptions. Dilah may marry to ensure hir baby is born legitimately, but after the birth, s/he wants to go back to being a *hunter*. Dilah's deliberations show that ideology does indeed fashion individual behavior but that it is not totally encompassing—negotiation, and even resistance, is still an option.

Ance'

When I first met Ance', s/he was 34 years old. Hir experience of gender norms is complex. When s/he was growing up, s/he was taught that as a girl, s/he would some day marry a man and have children. But even at a young age, s/he did not feel entirely comfortable with the future society had mapped out for hir. Society assumed that s/he would naturally follow gender norms, but for Ance' there was nothing natural about becoming a wife. Hir earliest experiences of defying gender expectations were that s/he did not like playing with other girls or having long hair. Ance' did not like doing any of the things a girl is supposed to do in order to learn what being a woman entails. Indeed, Ance' did not like helping hir mother and sisters in the kitchen, and s/he always found excuses to go and help hir father or follow hir brothers on some adventure. This behavior was tolerated when s/he was young, but as s/he got older, more and more pressure was placed on hir to be a proper woman; particularly, there was a lot of pressure on hir to get married. Like Dilah, Ance' wanted to have children but s/he neither wanted to marry a man nor follow the strict model of womanhood that was expected of hir.

Ance' thought a lot about how s/he could have children within Bugis society. S/he knew that the only legitimate way for her to have a baby would be by marrying a man, but s/he also knew that s/he would find it almost impossible to uphold feminine ideals of being a wife. The outcomes of hir deliberations are certainly innovative and, given the circumstances, perfectly logical. Ance' married a calabai. Hir spouse, Wawal, was male-bodied but followed a set of gender codes closely associated with feminine ideals. When Ance' told me this, I must have looked rather surprised because hir aunt said to the lady sitting next to her, "Look here, Puang, this *bule* just can't believe that a calalai and a calabai could possibly marry." But this option allowed Ance' to legitimately have children, and it enabled hir to continue masculine activities.

In a way, Ance' and Wawal maintained dominant gender norms in their marriage. There was a masculine and a feminine partner; Ance' took on the roles of a husband, and Wawal took on the roles of a wife. Of course, though, there were certain biological imperatives that continued to dictate certain roles; for instance, Ance' gave birth to their daughter.

This account reveals two key things: the agency of Ance' and the strength of dominant gender ideology. Ance' could not see any other options available to hir apart from being either a feminine wife or masculine husband. Ance' wanted to be the masculine husband, so s/he needed someone to assume the other half of the relationship, the feminine wife. So while Ance' and Wawal certainly subverted ideal gender norms, their relationship continued to uphold binary gender codes.

Maman

I heard from a number of different sources of a calalai who lived in a village just north of Sengkang. One morning I went to the bus station and found a bus heading to that village. Eventually we came to a small hamlet, and the bus driver yelled out, "*Sudah! Sudah sampai* (We're here)." I alighted in what felt like the middle of

nowhere, walked over to a *warung* (a small food stall), and hesitantly asked if anyone knew of any females who were like men. A younger couple who had just
finished eating their *bakso* (meatball soup) kindly offered to take me to Maman's
house. Maman, they said, was female and s/he was just like a man.

We shortly arrived at a typical Bugis house, and my companions indicated
that I should climb the stairs. It felt so intrusive and invasive, just wandering
into someone's house, asking if any calalai lived there. Timidly, I climbed up.
At the top, an elderly man greeted me and introduced himself as Maman's father,
Pak Syamsuryadi—word obviously traveled quickly in this village. Pak Syamsuryadi told me Maman was out in the fields harvesting rice. He asked if I wanted to
go out and meet hir or if I would rather come in and have a cup of tea and some
cake and wait for Maman to come home. It was the middle of the day, searing
hot, and no one was particularly clear on which rice field Maman was actually
in. I thought about Maman's father having to walk me around various rice fields
and the fact that we may not even find hir. I also wondered what I would say to
Maman in the middle of a field. A cup of tea sounded very tempting.

Pak Syamsuryadi told me that while Maman lives with him, more often than
not Maman is out traveling around. Pak Syamsuryadi is very proud of this fact and
mentioned that Maman travels so much because s/he is good at initiating business
ventures. While hir father hinted at the large amount of money Maman made,
their house was anything but luxurious. The only furniture in the small, hot
front room was a stiff couch. The only decorations were photos of Maman.

In every respect, Maman looked exactly like a man. In all the photos, hir
short hair was slicked back and s/he wore dark mirror sunglasses, denim jeans,
and a jacket. In one photo, s/he was surrounded by individuals I took to be
men. In another photo, there was a pretty woman wearing a red dress with her
arm slung casually over Maman's shoulder. Maman's father noticed me staring
at the photos, and he confirmed my suspicion that this was indeed Maman. He
then told me that Maman often goes to Java, and when s/he is there s/he
makes a lot of money. Pak Syamsuryadi used the term **berani** (brave) to describe
Maman and hir extensive travels; this is striking because *berani* is an adjective usually reserved for men. Maman's father then foraged for another photo of Maman,
and it was one where Maman was holding a lighted cigarette, straddling a motor-
cycle, hand on chin, elbow on knee.

Pak Syamsuryadi told me that Maman has always been masculine, and while
s/he is female, he knows that for many people this is not obvious. Ever since Pak
Syamsuryadi can remember, Maman was like a son. Indeed, Pak Syamsuryadi said
he always treated Maman like a son. Maman's mother left when Maman was quite
young, so Maman became particularly close to hir father. Maman and hir father
worked together as blacksmiths for a long time, but Maman's father lamented that
he is too old now to work, and he has to be supported by Maman.

Shortly after Pak Syamsuryadi finished telling me a bit about Maman, I heard
someone making her way up the rickety stairs. The woman who came in looked
just like the woman in the red dress in the photo. As she came in, Pak Syamsuryadi introduced her as Mina, Maman's ex-girlfriend. It struck me as interesting
that the fact that Mina and Maman were once dating (**pacaran**) was

acknowledged so openly. The three of us, as well as some children who had earlier seated themselves at our feet, made our way out onto the veranda. As the formalities were over, I did not need to be entertained in the formal sitting room any longer, and we could take advantage of the breeze on the veranda. The arrival of tea and cake also helped to relax the atmosphere.

Maman's father sat off to the side, and Mina and I, surrounded now by a group of other people, including the couple who had escorted me there, started chatting. I talked a little about my research, saying that I was interested in Bugis culture and also about men and women and calalai and calabai. I was then told about many interesting aspects of Bugis culture, as the people there were all eager that I learn about Bugis ways. When the conversation abated, I asked Mina about Maman.

Mina told me that Maman was a blacksmith (**pandai besi**) and that Maman used to work with hir father, but, winking at Pak Syamsuryadi, Mina said he was too old now to work. Mina mentioned that blacksmithing is really hot work and that you have to sit in front of a kiln and hit the iron into shape and then sharpen it. Mina works in the rice fields, and while this is hard work, she acknowledges that it is not as hard as blacksmithing. Here Mina is alluding to the masculine nature of blacksmithing. Indeed, Mina then said that Maman is in essence just like a man (*pokoknya seperti lelaki*).

Mina talked about hir relationship with Maman in front of all the people on the veranda. I could not detect any sense of discomfort or embarrassment from either Mina or the other people. Mina presented Maman as hard working and pursuing an occupation that symbolized masculinity. After Mina and Maman had been together for a few years, though, Mina was arranged to marry a man, and consequently she had to break off her relationship with Maman. Mina said that Maman now has many new girlfriends upon whom s/he bestows gifts, affirming the wealth Maman has accumulated. By buying gifts, working as a blacksmith, and traveling great distances on hir own, Maman emulates Bugis ideals of masculinity and presents a form of calalai gender.

Gender Flexibility

There is flexibility in gender performances, despite the often apparent strictness of Bugis gender codes. I remember traveling to Makassar one day and stopping at a gas station along the way. My supervisor, Greg, was visiting me—I was lucky enough to have both of my supervisors come and stay with me during fieldwork—and he noticed that of the four pump attendants, two were women. The women had oily rags tied around their faces, and they were wearing tracksuits. I asked one of the passengers next to me if the pump attendants were calalai because to me this type of work was a stark contrast to the type of work Bugis women should ideally do. Indeed, a man called Pak Rudin had recently told me that Bugis women are not like Balinese women, who have to work on the roads. Bugis women are honored and respected, he said; if there is dirty work that needs doing, men do it. Another man, Haji Ismail, had also said that more Bugis women go on the hajj to Mecca than men because Bugis men honor their wives so much that they make sure their wives go first. However, the passenger in the car replied that the women pumping gas were just average women (**wanita biasa**), not calalai or rough women (**wanita kasar**); they were just women doing their job. Women, then, can do masculine tasks, and indeed calalai can appear feminine.

On the morning of January 12, 2000, I received a card from Dilah. It was the festive season, both for Muslims (Idul Fitri, the end of the fasting month, Ramadan) and for Christians (Christmas, New Year), so I was not surprised to receive a season's greeting card. What was unusual, though, was the English inscription in the card:

> As you celebrate your anniversary
> May all the memories you have saved
> Since your wedding day
> Make this a very special time
> You'll want to last forever
> A lovely way to celebrate the life you've built together
> Happy Anniversary!

I mention this card not so much for the curious inscription but because of the way in which Dilah wrote hir personal note. As a calalai, Dilah is publicly against all things popularly considered feminine, although s/he is very nurturing with hir nieces and nephews. It struck me, then, that s/he had written a personal note in gold pen with squiggly writing and that the card was adorned with kisses. The card was decorated in such a way to suggest it was written by a teenage girl, rather than a 30-year-old calalai. So there is certainly fusion between masculine and feminine elements in calalai identity, and flexibility in gender performances.

SEXUALITY

Among some calalai and their partners, and indeed among many people in Bugis society, there is an expectation that any sexual activity will mirror heterosexual behavior. As a result, many people assume that calalai perform the role of a sexually insertive partner. Puang Bachri, a middle-aged man, asked me once if I knew how calalai have sex with women. When asked, I shook my head, and he told me that calalai use a special tool (**alat**) for having sex. Nowadays, he said, they use a condom filled with some kind of substance, but a long time ago they would fill the lining of an animal's stomach. Sometimes, Puang Bachri said, they would make it long enough so they could both use it at the same time, and this was called a **loloni** (B). Other words I heard for dildo included **lasogatta** (B, rubber penis), and **to'ol to'olan**. Puang Bachri could only conceive of calalai having penetrative sex with their partners.

It was a point of concern for some people that, being female, calalai do not have the anatomical "tools" to have penetrative sex. Yulia, whom you will meet in Chapter 5, is a 33-year-old calabai, and s/he used the fact that calalai lack a penis to undermine calalai status. S/he told me that it is a sin for a calalai and a woman to have sex. When I questioned hir about this, reminding hir that s/he has told me that s/he does not think it is a sin for a calabai to have sex with a man, s/he said that it is a sin because God has not given calalai the *alat* to have penetrative sex. Calalai themselves, though, do not necessarily feel they have to emulate perceptions of heterosexuality.

Once when I was receiving a *crem-bath* from Dilah at the salon where s/he worked, a woman walked past us. Dilah commented that the woman was very cute (*manis sekali*). When I agreed, Dilah told me that hir ex-girlfriend, Nisma, looked just like her. Dilah said that when the two of them met, Nisma was married to a man and that the couple had a child. But Dilah noted that Nisma was already ill (*sakit*, i.e., had same-sex sexual desires) before she got married but that she was forced to marry anyway. Before Dilah met Nisma, s/he used to fantasize about lots of sexy women (*cewek yang bahenol*), just like a man, but when s/he met Nisma, Dilah knew that she wanted to be in a long-term steady relationship with her. When they were living together Dilah told me they had sex about three times a week, sometimes using a vibrator. Dilah noted that both *hunter* and *lines* are penetrated, but it depended on the people and the mood. If they had planned to have sex, then maybe they used a vibrator; if it just happened, then maybe they did not use any tool at all.

Dilah acknowledged that like with any couple, sexual relationships differ; sometimes they had sex a lot, sometimes not very often. It depended on what was happening and how they felt. Dilah said, though, that *hunter* do not really focus on sex. For Dilah, giving love and affection (*kasih sayang*) is a much more important foundation on which to build a relationship than just sex. For Dilah, calalai sexuality is not defined solely by following imagined norms of heterosexuality, where calalai are expected to take a masculine penetrative role.

Calalai relationships with *lines* challenge norms of heterosexuality and heteronormativity. Dilah defines a *lines* as a female who feels like a woman but who is not sexually attracted to men. Rather, *lines* sexually desire and like hanging around with females who have the style of men. *Lines* challenge gender norms often more subversively than calalai, and in some ways, *lines* destabilize calalai assertions of masculinity. Dilah once told me that *lines* are the most assertive partner and that they are always the first to ask for sex. This behavior contradicts the gender norm that men are sexually assertive and women are sexually receptive. *Lines* flaunt femininity; they are often exquisitely dressed with well-applied make-up. Yet *lines* refuse to abide by many of the prescriptions applied to women. For instance, *lines* often demand freedom to travel around on their own and to wear short skirts, and they are sexually assertive. *Lines* may be married to men and have children, but they find emotional and sexual satisfaction with calalai. Calalai sexuality, then, does not necessarily follow ideals of masculine heterosexuality.

COMMUNITY REACTIONS

How are calalai viewed within the social setting in which they live? It is true that calalai subjectivity is often officially discouraged and that same-sex sexual desire is commonly perceived as a type of illness, even by calalai themselves.

However, calalai tend to be tolerated and, within their home communities, even accepted.

When I asked Dilah about how society perceives hir gender identity, s/he said that s/he does not tend to get hassled for being a masculine female. Occasionally s/he gets comments like, "Who are you?" or "Why are you so rough (*kasar*)?" However, Dilah has never been attacked or threatened or particularly teased. While certainly the lack of violence should not suggest there is acceptance of calalai, it does imply a relatively high level of tolerance.

People are often shocked to discover that calalai are female, as calalai are frequently assumed to be male. Terms of address are important in Indonesian conversation, so soon after I met Eri, a calalai in hir early 20s who works in the same beauty salon as Dilah, I asked hir how I should address hir, as **Mbak** (Miss) or **Mas** (Mr). Eri replied that for hir it is not really important. S/he prefers to be called by hir first name, without adding *Mbak* or *Mas* in front of it. Eri said that s/he often gets called *Mas* though. S/he recounted one story where a woman came into the salon and Eri cut her hair. The woman kept calling Eri *Mas*, and Eri did not make any comment. At the end of the session, Eri was massaging hir client's arms when the woman grabbed Eri's hand, exclaiming, "Wow! Your hands are so soft. Oh my God, you're a gal (*cewek*)!"

The woman was more shocked than angry at finding out that Eri was female. However, the woman did express pity toward Eri. In the woman's view, Eri would never find happiness. Happiness, the woman believed, was found through heterosexual marriage, bearing children, and conforming to gender norms. Indeed, it is emotions such as pity that are more commonly leveled at calalai than animosity.

To some extent, calalai find a support base within calabai circles. For instance, at Festival Waria, a dancing and beauty festival held annually for *waria*, there are bound to be calalai in attendance. Furthermore, at the beauty salon where Dilah works, calabai and calalai work together in a supportive environment. Andi Lutfi further told me that calalai and calabai get along together and that they give support to each other. One of the most striking instances that I witnessed of the camaraderie between calalai and calabai was at a nightclub called M Klub. I arrived there late one night and wandered around trying to find Dilah. Eventually, Dilah called my name over the microphone because s/he was up on the stage and could see me trying to find hir. I made my way over to hir and was greeted by a number of other calalai, *lines*, and calabai who were all dancing—Eri was the DJ. I met a calabai I had not met before named Fari. Fari was dressed in a miniskirt, hir head was shaved, and s/he had recently had silicone pumped into hir nose—Fari was very proud of the bruise that this had left. Shortly after my arrival, a competition was announced called "Who Has the Most Gorgeous Partner?" Dilah encouraged, and literally pushed, Fari to run to the other end of the stage. When Fari got there, s/he pulled out a photo of hir boyfriend. The boyfriend was particularly handsome, but he could not compete with a boyfriend in the flesh, so Fari did not win the competition. What struck me most, though, was that a calalai was being supportive of a calabai.

While there is usually persistent pressure on calalai to marry and have children, many calalai do receive acceptance and support from their community.

We cannot, then, focus just on the negative attitudes expressed toward calalai from within official teachings or on the derogatory comments and actions made by some individuals. Moreover, we should not just focus on the positive attitudes expressed in the everyday tolerance extended to calalai. In reality, there are a variety of reactions expressed toward calalai, and there are a multitude of experiences felt by calalai.

CONCLUSION

There is a lot of pressure placed on female-born individuals in Bugis South Sulawesi to conform to models of ideal femininity. As a result, few individuals identify themselves as calalai, as the first part of this chapter revealed. Dilah, Ance', and Maman are exceptions, and their stories are recounted throughout this chapter. Through their experiences, we heard of ways in which calalai emulate some aspects of ideal masculinity. For instance, Maman works as a blacksmith, travels alone throughout the archipelago, and uses hir financial earnings to buys gifts for hir girlfriends. In other ways, though, calalai challenge masculine norms. Dilah talks of how *lines* are the most sexually assertive partner, thus defying the expectation that women are the sexually passive and receptive partner in sexual relationships. In the narratives of Ance', we saw how certain levels of negotiation are possible. While Ance' accepted that s/he had to marry a male in order to legitimately have children, within hir marriage s/he maintained hir life as a masculine female.

This chapter also examined social responses to calalai. While theoretically calalai identity is disapproved of, where calalai are known in a particular community they tend not to experience overt hostility, at least when they become productive members of the community. There is, however, continuing pressure on calalai to marry and have children, at least until calalai are in their late 30s. By embodying some aspects of masculinity, calalai find an avenue through which they can enact masculine behavior and pursue same-sex desires. Yet, calalai identity is not constructed entirely on masculine or heterosexual models; rather, Dilah, Ance', and Maman demand recognition as calalai.

ENDNOTE

1. Readers may wonder why no photos of calalai appear in this case study. While some calalai expressly said they did not want their photo to be published, other calalai did give their permission. Unfortunately, though, I do not have any suitable photos of individuals who gave their permission.

5

Male Transgendering

YULIA'S BIRTHDAY: A PRELUDE

As Yulia and I share the same birth date, s/he kindly invited me to come and share in hir very elaborate birthday celebration. So at 3 p.m. yesterday, Yulia came and collected me and we went to hir house. When we arrived, there were a number of calabai waiting for us, including Yanti and hir boyfriend.

Yulia, as expected, had planned a huge party. I was anticipating that the party would be held at Yulia's house, but of course it would never have accommodated the hundreds of people s/he had invited. So instead Yulia hired a tent; the birthday party looked as elaborate as a wedding. The preparations for the party had taken place over the last few months but most particularly in the last three days, when food preparation was undertaken.

Just after 4 p.m., Yulia decided it was time to start getting ready. Yulia, Yanti, and I went into Yulia's bedroom, and Yanti started doing Yulia's makeup. There were some young girls who had been running in and out of the house, and they came into Yulia's bedroom just as s/he was almost ready and told Yulia that s/he looked very pretty (cantik sekali). At about 6 p.m. we all went downstairs to the tent where the party was. Yulia sat at the head table facing many rows of chairs. Three of Yulia's nieces also share similar birth dates, so they were celebrating too. Yulia had made them all matching pink dresses, just like hers, and their own multilayered cake with candles.

As people arrived, they went up to the head table and greeted Yulia and passed hir envelopes of money. It was like Yulia was a bride, as this is what happens at weddings; Yulia even looked as stunning as a bride in hir evening gown. After Yulia had received the guests, we all started eating from the extensive buffet. When people had finished the main course, we moved on to dessert—this is the reverse of many Bugis celebrations where people eat sweets before eating savory food. After dessert it was time for cake. All the village children who had been unable to squeeze in for the buffet came into the tent to get a piece.

There were more cakes and more people at Yulia's party than at any Sengkang wedding I have been to. There must have been 500 people attending over the course of the evening. There were about 60 calabai present, and they sat together on one side of the tent, and the children and adults sat on the other side. The people who did not get a seat stood at the back of the tent. While there was a spatial difference between calabai and everyone else, there was constant interaction. Calabai served noncalabai friends food; men and women went over and chatted with calabai, and calabai went to the other side of the tent to talk with friends.

Calabai were dressed to the nines. Some calabai have amazing figures—lean, muscular legs, taut stomachs, long flowing hair—and they looked amazing in their ball gowns. Their over-the-top glamour is often the only way you can tell calabai from women, and the fact that they smoke like chimneys, which women should not do. Other calabai wore rather sexy clothing: short skirts, low-cut tops, and other apparel women could not really get away with wearing. Not all calabai presented such hyperfeminine images though. Some calabai simply wore jeans and t-shirts. Calabai who have been on the hajj have an obligation to wear men's clothes, so there were some calabai who, while wearing makeup, wore men's clothes and the peci, *which is a rimless Islamic cap—but they wore lurid, colored* peci, *so even calabai who have been on the hajj presented a unique appearance.*

After we had finished eating cake, Yanti's band began playing. Some people, mostly calabai and children, went up to the stage and started dancing. The last I saw of Yulia, s/he was looking very satisfied with how it was all going. (Field notes, 1999)

As we can see from this fieldnote extract, calabai often present feminine images; Yulia, for instance, wore a ball gown to hir party, s/he wore makeup, and hir long hair was elaborately presented. But it is not possible to consider that calabai are simply trying to emulate Bugis women; some calabai were dressed in short skirts and low-cut tops and they smoked cigarettes, all things Bugis women generally should not do. So rather than wanting to become women, calabai often actively present their own identity; thus, they are often considered a specific gender category in Bugis society. Of course, community reactions to calabai vary, and along with exploring calabai subjectivity, this chapter examines social perceptions of calabai.

Within Indonesia there are a number of terms used in relation to subjectivities similar to calabai. The most common national terms are *banci, bencong, wadam* (from *wanita adam,* "woman Adam," as in Adam and Eve), *walsu* (from *wanita palsu,* "false woman") and *waria* (from *wanita pria,* "woman man"). In this book, I use the term *calabai* for two reasons. First, there is no singular term that all people use, so whichever term I chose would not be representative of everyone, although *waria* is arguably the most widely used polite term. Second, there are differences between *waria* identity and calabai identity. For instance, many calabai in Bugis South Sulawesi have an institutional role as wedding mothers (*Indo' Botting*—a role that is discussed in Chapter 7) that *waria* elsewhere do not have. Calabai identity is certainly not a purely localized identity. For instance, Yulia's interaction with transgendered males in Malaysia had a significant influence on hir approach to gender. However, for many individuals their gendered performances are very much situated in Bugis

South Sulawesi. Etymologically, calabai means "false woman," but we should not assume that this means calabai are women impersonators. As this chapter shows, we should take the term *calabai* to indicate biological males who enact a type of femininity that Bugis women do not perform.

MALE FEMININITY

Eka's Femininity

Eka runs hir own hair salon, which s/he operates at the front of hir parent's house. Although s/he was just 25 years old when I first met hir, s/he already had a successful business. At busy times, for instance during the wedding season, Eka employs two calabai friends to assist hir with the workload. Eka's appearance is in many ways very feminine. S/he has long black hair, s/he wears makeup, and hir eyebrows are meticulously shaped. Hir clothing choices often consist of tight, low-cut tops; mini-skirts; and high-heeled shoes. Hir gait is swaying, s/he is delicate in hir gestures, and s/he is soft spoken. To a foreign observer, Eka may appear to exude femininity, but this type of femininity differs from more localized images of femininity, as discussed in chapter three.

Eka also feels like a woman in many ways. I often went to Eka's salon to get a massage. The first time I went there, Eka directed me into a small room that had a mattress on the floor. When s/he asked me to remove my clothes to facilitate the massage, I hesitated; Eka was, after all, male. Eka sensed my anxiety and said that I did not have to worry because no men would come in. I must have still looked worried because Eka added that I did not need to be shy (**jangan malu**) because we were both women (*wanita*). Eka said that we are both the same in our hearts; it is only parts of our physical bodies that are different, and s/he pointed to hir genitals. Eka did not dismiss hir male body, but s/he indicated that inside, where for hir it counts, s/he felt like a woman.

I never heard Eka express the idea of being a woman trapped inside a man's body, however. In fact the few times I did hear such sentiments were from people who had experience of the West. The particular understanding of gender in Bugis South Sulawesi, as discussed in Chapter 2, generally precludes the idea of having a body that is incompatible with your gender; gender is in part constituted through the body. As such, a feminine-male can be considered a separate gender. However, just because the male body is never forgotten does not mean that calabai do not manipulate their body so it more closely resembles a woman's. Indeed, Yulia has undertaken procedures to feminize hir body, as we will now see.

Yulia's Femininity

The success and glamour of Yulia's birthday party was not just a stroke of luck. S/he is one of the most respected wedding organizers in Sengkang and, as such, has had a lot of experience in arranging social events. Yulia is a skilled makeup artist and dressmaker, and hir services are highly sought after, not just in Sengkang but further afield. Yulia is economically successful, and s/he has saved enough money to buy hir own house. Built in typical Bugis style, Yulia's stilt house (*bola riase'*, B) has three sections. The front section is where guests are received. The middle section is where Yulia sleeps and does dressmaking, while the back section forms the kitchen.

The community in which Yulia lives, a tiny hamlet five kilometers from the center of Sengkang, is a tight-knit one. If I ever went to visit Yulia and s/he was not there, someone could always tell me where s/he was. Yulia spends much of hir time at hir aunt's house, which is just up the path from Yulia's house; this is where Yulia's three nieces live, and often they patiently act as models for Yulia to practice hir makeup, hair styling, and dressmaking skills.

Yulia's male name begins with *Andi,* a Bugis title indicating high status. Yulia's social position meant that hir parents felt great shame (*siri'*, B) when they found out s/he was calabai. Along with status, kinship is also very important in Bugis society, and because hir parents assumed that Yulia would not produce any legitimate heirs, hir parents were doubly shamed. Being calabai certainly does not necessarily preclude future heterosexual marriage and children, but the common perception is that it does. The feeling of *siri'* Yulia's parents felt was so great that they left Sengkang. This exodus suggests that gender ideals are more strictly attached to members of the noble class than to other members of society.

Feminizing the Body

Yulia acknowledges that s/he was born male but s/he still wishes to feminize hir body. During my fieldwork, Yulia went to live in Malaysia, and while s/he was there s/he developed a strong desire to manipulate hir body:

> When I got back from attending a wedding in Jakarta, I was really looking forward to seeing Yulia again, but s/he had taken off to Malaysia. Hir family told me s/he would be away for a couple of weeks, but it has been three months—ya ampun (have mercy)! This morning I went again to Yulia's house, hoping s/he had finally come home, but hir family said s/he was still away. So I was quite surprised when at 4 p.m. today there was a knock on my bedroom door and it was Yulia!
>
> Yulia has dyed hir hair bright red and s/he was wearing sunglasses. In hir own words, s/he looked, "persis cewek bule (just like a Western chick)." S/he is living in Malaysia now, s/he said, and has just come back to get the rest of hir belongings. We sat down and s/he started telling me about Malaysia. Yulia said that in Malaysia lots of waria are having breast enhancement surgery, and some of the implants they are getting are bigger than coconuts! It is quite an expensive operation though, at around Rp1.2 million (US$120); a civil servant earns around half that per month. S/he said calabai are also getting silicone injected into their noses to make them more prominent (lebih mancung). Yulia showed me a pin-sized bruise at the top of her nose where s/he has just had four injections (disuntik). S/he has also had silicone injected into hir chin and lips. Silicone injections are relatively cheap at around Rp30,000 (US$3). Yulia told me that

some calabai are having sex-reassignment surgery. If the cost was not prohibitive, Yulia said s/he would like to get this done, and s/he would also like to have breast implants, but together it would cost around Rp17 million (US$1,700). S/he said s/he is brave enough and that s/he has the desire to do it; s/he just needs the cash (duit). (Field notes, 1999)

Yulia, fresh from hir travels overseas, expressed a desire for radical feminizing surgery. A primary reason why calabai aim to feminize their bodies is to make themselves look more feminine and hence, in their eyes, more beautiful. The more beautiful they are, the easier they perceive it will be to attract men.

Some calabai desire such surgery not just for aesthetic reasons but because of the perceived financial reward. After sex-reassignment surgery, calabai sex workers can earn up to Rp250,000 (US$25) a night, while before the operation they earn only about Rp50,000 (US$5). *Waria* in Jakarta have established their own **arisan** in response to the high cost of sex-reassignment surgery. An *arisan* is a social gathering held monthly where members contribute to, and take turns at winning, a combined sum of money through a lottery system. This money can then be used for sex-reassignment surgery. Loyalty to the *arisan* is such that no *waria* has yet run off after winning the lottery—if *waria* involved in sex work did leave the group after winning, they would be forbidden by other *waria* from working on the streets.

While Yulia and some *waria* in urban centers such as Jakarta express a desire to undergo feminizing surgery, I did not meet many calabai in Bugis South Sulawesi who wanted to undertake such radical procedures. The high cost of the operation is certainly a prohibitive factor, but more commonly the reason given for not desiring surgery is that calabai do not see their genitalia as being at odds with their idea of self—recall Chapter 2 where some calabai revealed that their fate is to be feminine males.

While calabai tend to not want radical surgery, most calabai do feminize their physical body in some way. Indeed, calabai who make no effort at feminizing their presentation may be derided by other calabai with snide remarks such as, "Where's ya tits (*tete' mu di mana loh*)?"

A rather vivacious calabai in hir early 20s, named Tilly, frequently sits around plucking facial hair with a pair of tweezers attached to hir keyring. Tilly told me that s/he takes hormone tablets, primarily the Pill, to make hir breasts larger and hir voice higher pitched. Tilly also injects silicone into hir hips to make them rounder. Other areas where silicone is commonly injected include the nose, cheeks, lips, breasts, and buttocks.

Feminizing Appearance and Roles

Attempts to achieve femininity do not stop at the physical body. Calabai dress in feminine clothing such as short skirts, often following perceived Western images rather than Bugis images of femininity, such as *sarong*. Calabai tend to grow their hair long and wear at least some makeup each day. Beauty, appearance, glamour, and style are all important in calabai constructions of identity (Figures 5.1, 5.2, 5.3).

FIGURE 5.1 Calabai getting ready for a party

FIGURE 5.2 Calabai getting ready for a party

FIGURE 5.3 Calabai getting ready for a party

Features of Indonesian ideals of womanhood are also taken on by calabai. The Indonesian nation is based on a family principle (*azas kekeluargaan*). The nuclear family, with the man as husband, father, and head of the family, and the woman as wife and mother, is the favored model, as we saw in Chapter 3. One way in which calabai negotiate this norm is by assuming the role of wife in romantic relationships. In effecting this, calabai occasionally marry their male partners in a ceremony known as "marriage below the hand" (*kawin di bawah tangan*)—this phrase is also used for partners in de facto relationships and sometimes for polygamous marriages.

Yanti is now in hir late 40s, but when s/he was younger, s/he was "married" to a man. Hir husband was a technician in the band in which s/he sang. Yanti saw this marriage as a particularly good match as the two of them would perform together at weddings, birthdays, and Independence Day celebrations. Yanti would sing all types of songs, particularly jazz and **dangdut**—dangdut is a genre of Indonesian popular music partly derived from a mix of Arab, Indian, and Malay folk music. The couple were married for a number of years, and while they were married Yanti said s/he was exactly like a wife and as such s/he did all the cooking and cleaning and raised their adopted son. But the couple eventually separated because Yanti considered they were no longer suitable (*cocok*) for each other. While it lasted, Yanti's marriage mirrored a heteronormative relationship in many ways. Following this model provided Yanti with some social legitimacy because in a sense hir relationship followed accepted marital norms. Yulia, as we will see now, also entered into a relationship with a man and assumed the role of wife, although s/he more precisely became a "kept woman."

Sexual Femininity

The reason Yulia went to Malaysia was because s/he met a Caucasian foreigner (*bule*) named Steve, and he convinced hir to come and live near him; indeed, Steve gave Yulia Rp5 million (US$500) to come back to Sengkang to collect the rest of hir belongings. When Yulia came and saw me after returning from Malaysia, s/he was full of news about hir new life and hir new man.

Yulia had never been out with a *bule* before s/he met Steve, but s/he was instantly attracted to him. Not only was Steve handsome but he was very kind-hearted. Steve asked Yulia to become a Christian, but Yulia declined because for hir it does not matter what religion people are as long as they respect each other. Moreover, Yulia worried that if Steve eventually left hir, s/he would be unable to become a Muslim again.

Yulia and Steve met in Jakarta. Yulia does not know which country he is from, and when I asked what s/he did know about him, s/he said that he's circumcised (*disunat*), he's tall (*tinggi*), he's thin (*kurus*), and he's bald (*botak*). Yulia said that Steve is married to a woman and they have children together, but Steve told hir that they have separated.

Shortly after they met, Yulia and Steve worked out a five-year contract. During this time, Yulia will be paid between Rp1–3 million (US$100–US$300) per month. On top of this, Steve pays for hir accommodation in Malaysia at a type of boarding house (*kos*), which comes to Rp1 million (US$100) per month. Yulia does not need to cook or clean or do anything in terms of hir own upkeep. In return for all of this, Yulia needs to be sexually available to Steve. In Yulia's words, "All I have to do is play with him at night!" Yulia recognizes that their contract will depend on whether they continue to be suitable (*cocok*) together. Yulia admits that Steve might get sick of hir before the five years is up, but Steve has assured hir that s/he is too sweet to get tired of.

Romantic relationships between calabai and their partners sometimes reflect normative gender models where men economically provide for their spouses; for instance, Yulia is financially taken care of by Steve. But it is not just the financial heterosexual model that some calabai–man relationships mirror; popularly espoused models may also be followed in sexual relationships as well.

When I asked about sex, Yulia was adamant that hir partners, including Steve, are never sexually penetrated. Rather, Yulia said that it is calabai who are sexually penetrated. Yulia symbolized sexual penetration by poking hir thumb between hir first and second fingers. Another symbol used to express male–male sex is made by placing one hand on top of the other, palms down, and rotating the thumbs. If Yulia did penetrate Steve, s/he would consider this behavior to be lesbian (*itu namanya lesbian*). I am not entirely sure what Yulia meant by the term *lesbian* here, but as I discussed in Chapter 2, s/he probably sees such activities as signifying a homogender relationship, which is not generally accepted in Bugis society. At one point in this particular conversation about sex, Yulia hinted that it was getting too personal and that we should stop talking about it. Just as I was about to raise another topic, Yulia got up off my bed, looked at me, and animatedly told me that Steve's penis (*kontol*) was enormous. To emphasize the point, Yulia strode over to my dresser and picked up my roll-on deodorant, indicating that Steve's penis was even bigger than that.

In some ways, calabai–men relationships resemble heteronormative relationships, with calabai assuming the roles of a wife or mistress and being the receptive partner in sexual relations. Calabai also take on aspects of femininity by wearing women's clothing (influenced both by national and international trends), applying makeup, and growing their hair long. Calalai also feminize their physical body through surgery, silicone injections, the ingestion of hormone tablets, and hair removal. In other ways, though, calabai challenge feminine ideals, disrupt the gender binaries of female-feminine women and male-masculine men, and affirm their own gendered identity.

CALABAI GENDER

Gender Play

One day during my fieldwork, I went to a house where Yulia was preparing for a wedding ceremony. When I arrived, a woman led me through to the back of the house where Yulia was up to her elbows in cake mixture. The house was full of industrious people, so I found a piece of unoccupied floor out of the way and sat down. This was the groom's house, and the bride was expected there quite soon.

Within the hour everything was almost organized, so Yulia rewarded hirself with a quick break and came and sat next to me. Some other women and another calabai named Tilly also joined our circle. Quite out of the blue, Tilly announced that hir breasts were small. I read Tilly's comment as dissatisfaction with hir body, that s/he felt like a woman but because s/he had small breasts, s/he was not womanly. I responded to Tilly by reassuring hir that there is more to being feminine than large breasts and, by way of emphasis, I added that I too had small breasts. Tilly's retort was quite unexpected. S/he boasted that s/he was able to change the size of hir breasts at any time s/he wished simply by inserting more padding, and if s/he ever needed to wash them, s/he could just take them out. At that point, Tilly removed a piece of foam cut in the shape of a breast from hir bra and waved it around. Everyone started laughing.

Through hir actions Tilly parodied femaleness, and hir antics showed a sense of gender play. Breasts are a way of signifying femininity, and this is why Tilly wears a padded bra and why a calabai who does not wear a bra may be derided by hir friends. But Tilly removed hir "breasts" to show that s/he is not female but that s/he can have fun with femininity.

It might be said that calabai work so hard at achieving femininity because of their contested gender status. It might also be said that calabai consciously overdo femininity to emphasize a distinct gender identity. Most calabai do not desire or intend to pass as women, and they are rarely read as women. If calabai wanted to

FIGURE 5.4 A calabai fashion parade

be considered women, they would need to model themselves more on local images of femininity, which ideally require individuals to be reserved and demure, as we saw in Chapter 3. Instead, calabai manipulate Western notions of contemporary femininity, to an extent Bugis women rarely do, and images from international Mardi Gras parades and drag queen performances. What results from calabai mixing local and international influences is calabai producing innovative fashions, elaborate hairstyles, and campy behavior and appearance, mostly publicly seen in fashion parades (Figure 5.4). This performance accords calabai a distinct gendered space in Bugis South Sulawesi.

Calabai Entertainment

Calabai are often in demand to perform at weddings, birthday parties, and cultural festivals. Their preoccupation with appearance means that people often look to calabai for new fashion styles, and their performances are often very entertaining. Calabai performances may also provide examples of how women and men should not behave.

There are many festivals in Bugis society, and at these festivals school students, Islamic groups, and calabai often perform together. While school groups get proud claps of support, it is calabai groups who receive the most raucous applause—as seen at the festival recounted in Chapter 2. At one particular festival held at the bus station, where most festivals in Sengkang are held, the crowd was so dense that I had to go right to the front to get a clear view. When the calabai group came on, the crowd went wild. The calabai wore sexy clothing (e.g., miniskirts), and their routine incorporated a lot of slapstick humor. Calabai did pelvic thrusts toward the audience and bent over to show fluffy pink panties. The band that followed the calabai received a very different response. The female singer was dressed in similar attire to the calabai, including platform high-heeled shoes, a short skirt, and a tiny tank top. She did similar dance moves to the calabai, but she stopped short of revealing her underwear. While the calabai had drawn the crowd in and their performances incited shouts of joviality, when the woman started singing and dancing, there was a mass exodus of people and a large space in front of the stage was cleared. I do not think the exodus was the result of the band's performance; the woman was a good singer and performer. I read the exodus of people as a sign of their disapproval. There was endorsement for calabai to wear sexy clothes and do sexy moves; the crowd closed in, people clapped, cheered, and cajoled. For the woman, however, there appeared to be condemnation; a woman should be modest and demure, not outlandish. Calabai are rewarded for behavior that women are discouraged from emulating.

Romantic Relationships

In a significant way, calabai–men relationships frequently differ from popular ideas of heterosexual relationships. One example of this is that calabai economically support their partners in almost all relationships in Sengkang.

I wrote earlier about Yulia's relationship with Steve, where Yulia is financially supported by hir partner. Yulia has never had a serious relationship with a man in Sengkang because s/he does not want to have the responsibility of financially supporting a man. Yulia was briefly seeing a man called Fajar in Sengkang, but Yulia said that all he was interested in was hir money, so Yulia ended that relationship. Yulia demands that hir boyfriends pay for hir living expenses, and the model of calabai–men relationships in Sengkang is for calabai to support the man.

Takrim, a 29-year-old man, told me that calabai are very generous. The partner of a calabai is given food and accommodation, he said, and bought clothes and cigarettes, and provided with entertainment. Calabai make especially attractive partners, Takrim told me, because often the man is "married off" (*dikasih kawin*) to a woman by their calabai partner.

In the serendipitous way that fieldwork often happens, a man named Pak Hidya unexpectedly came by one day and offered to take me to meet Sarimin, a calabai who makes a living by weaving sarongs on a wooden loom (Figure 5.5). On the way home from Sarimin's house, Pak Hidya said it was common practice for calabai to make a contract (*kontrak*) with a man to live with them for around three years—Pak Hidya was hinting that the man who lived with Sarimin was in such a contract. After this time, calabai arrange for the wedding (*menjodohkan*) of hir partner to a woman. If the man does not want to marry a woman, he can remain with his calabai partner, who will give him a substantial gift, like a motorbike, to secure the contract for a few more years.

Pak Hidya views relationships between calabai and men primarily as contractual agreements. Yulia also sees calabai–men relationships in Sengkang as

FIGURE 5.5 A calabai weaving silk sarong

financially motivated. Of course, many calabai–man relationships are based on affection and love (**kasih sayang**)—we also saw in Chapter 4 that for Dilah *kasih sayang* is the most important aspect in calalai–woman relationships. However, the common perception, which is not entirely undeserved, is that calabai–men relationships in Bugis South Sulawesi are primarily initiated and sustained by financial incentives. The fact that calabai are able to financially support their partners affirms that calabai tend to make a good living.

Calabai often have particular reasons for supporting their partner and for paying for their partner's wedding. Haji Sungke', an elderly bissu who works as a midwife (*dukun beranak*), told me that if calabai provide their partner (**sahabat**) with an elaborate wedding ceremony, then afterwards many handsome (*cakep*) men will be interested in that calabai. So, there can be self-interest in paying for a partner's wedding.

Haji Mappaganti is a 60-year-old calabai who works at a local school and is also the local scout leader. Haji Mappaganti paid for hir partner's wedding for a somewhat different reason. After many relationships with men, Haji Mappaganti became aware (*sadar*) that s/he had been wrong (i.e., committing a sin by having same-sex sexual relations). So Haji Mappaganti arranged the marriage of hir partner because s/he did not want him to continue committing a sin. After this, many men wanted to live with Haji Mappaganti, but s/he was bored with casual sex (*nyentot*) and did not want to continue to live life just for the pursuit of pleasure (*senang-senangan*). As we can see, then, there are different forms of romantic relationships between calabai and men and different motivations for such relationships, but most ostensibly conform to a particular model, that is, of calabai financially supporting their partner.

Attractions of Calabai

I was told of many reasons why men form relationships with calabai. Calabai are known to spoil (*manja*) their partners, and one young man named Jero' suggested that calabai are rather like "sugar daddies" who pay their partners for companionship and sex. Some people told me that men form romantic relationships with calabai because they, the men, have a particular inclination (*kecenderungan*) that makes them feel attracted to calabai. Nabilah, a civil servant in her mid-20s, said that calabai make attractive partners because the world opens up for you and you are given everything you could possibly need or want. When I asked Nabilah if true love is something that motivates calabai–men relationships, she said that while it may happen elsewhere, in South Sulawesi true love is rare. Nabilah believes relationships are about things other than romantic love. During one conversation, Nabilah wondered out loud what Yulia was doing in Malaysia. When I told her that Yulia was living with a *bule,* Nabilah confessed she had assumed Yulia was working as a *pelacur* (prostitute/hostess). Nabilah's assumption is a common one made when people hear of calabai working interstate or overseas. However, calabai who live in Sengkang tend not to be presumed to be involved in sex work—later in this chapter I recount such views espoused by the Provincial Secretary.

When Nabilah found out that Yulia was not working as a *pelacur,* she concluded that Yulia must be a *simpanan,* a term meaning "on the side," or "a storage," in this case connoting a mistress. It is not unheard of for married men to have a calabai *simpanan.* Nabilah said that men tend to get bored with their wives because their wives get older and they are no longer so attractive. A man may therefore find a calabai partner appealing because s/he is beautiful, s/he has a different body, s/he wears stunning clothing, and importantly, because s/he cannot get pregnant. Nabilah concluded by telling me that calabai can be good friends to women too and that calabai are fun to hang out with. But she warned me to watch out (*hati-hati*) and not to be alone in a room with a calabai because you never know if their man side will emerge (*muncul,* i.e., they might suddenly find women attractive)—we will hear more about the supposed capricious sexual desire of calabai later in this chapter.

In many ways, calabai contest ideal models of Bugis femininity and masculinity. By accepting their male body, although often altering it, choosing racy clothing and accoutrements, and providing for their male partner's well-being, calabai differentiate themselves from Bugis women and men and from popular models of heterosexual romantic relationships. By both emulating and contesting Bugis femininity and masculinity, calabai distort gender binaries and present a distinct gender identity.

SOCIAL PERCEPTIONS

There is no single view of calabai within Bugis South Sulawesi. Some people embrace calabai and the contribution they make to Bugis society through their role in weddings. Other people believe that calabai are living in sin. As a result of these different views, there are varying degrees of tolerance and acceptance for calabai. I want to first examine the extent to which calabai are considered in disparaging terms. Negative opinions of calabai extend primarily from the view of calabai as overly passionate individuals who neither embody restraint nor reason and from the view that calabai are committing a sin under Islam. Second, I want to explore more positive views of calabai, revealing that calabai are largely tolerated and even accepted within Bugis society.

Vacillating Passion and Anti-Calabai Sentiment

The ability to control your passions is a highly valued attribute in Bugis society—as we saw in Chapter 3, men are expected to embody reason and control their desires, and this makes men, rather than women, deserving of being *tau malise'*. There is a common perception, though, of calabai as individuals ruled by emotion, who are unable to be truthful, sensible, or rational.

Laly, a 22-year-old man, told me that calabai are habitual liars and that they even lie to themselves (*berbohong kepada diri sendiri*). Laly makes a strong moral condemnation of calabai subjectivity by suggesting calabai lie that they are women when they are not. Laly also believes calabai are prone to exaggeration (*hiperbola*). When calabai get together, they exaggerate (*melebih-lebihkan dan tambakan*) their stories, he said. For instance, a calabai might say that s/he spent the night in a hotel with a man, but in reality s/he just went for a walk with him. Laly thinks that in the past, calabai felt inferior (*merasa minder*) to the rest of society, so they kept to themselves. But because the post-Suharto era is more politically and socially relaxed than previous eras, calabai need not remain hidden. Solidarity-increasing measures like beauty pageants and the influence of gay consciousness in the West and surrounding regions have also meant that calabai are now more vocal and assertive in respect to their rights (Boellstorff, 2005). This is a worrying trend for Laly, as he has visions of calabai becoming too politically and economically powerful, which will lead Bugis society down a sinful path.

Jero', a 32-year-old man, gives another reason for not supporting calabai. Jero' believes calabai cannot control their passions and that they too quickly get jealous. If their partner starts to be interested in a woman, then the woman must watch out, Jero' said, because calabai possess potent magic that they will use to make the woman ill.

Calabai are also often believed to be unable to control their passions when it comes to sexual desire. Haji Baco', hirself a calabai and also a bissu, constantly warned me against traveling with Yulia and hir friends, especially when an overnight stay was involved. Haji Baco' feared that Yulia's man side (i.e., heterosexual desire) would surface, and s/he would try and seduce me—remember Nabilah also warned about this. Haji Baco' said that while calabai may publicly claim to only desire men, their man side can emerge at any time. This is a common perception of calabai, and some people even refer to calabai as AC/DC, suggesting they are sexually compatible with both men and women.

I was visiting Yulia one day when a number of calabai, women, and children were in hir house, all helping with certain aspects of cooking. Along with a few of the children, I was given the essential but relatively unskilled job of dipping saté sticks into peanut sauce. Tilly, the calabai who removed hir foam breast and shook it around, exclaimed how s/he was tired of men. All men do, s/he said, is kiss her, fuck (*nyentot*) her, then leave. Just as Tilly finished speaking, a child wandered over to us, and Tilly sat up straight and shook hir breasts at him. People laughed at Tilly's comments and behavior, perhaps as a way of dealing with hir contravention of polite conversation. While no one said or did anything to suggest umbrage at Tilly's actions, Tilly's unrestrained sexual expression often consigns hir to a social position of reserved tolerance.

Calabai are regularly perceived to be exhibitionists and promiscuous and to have a fondness for revealing intimate details of their sexual adventures to anyone who will listen. Such indecorous behavior is in stark contrast to what Bugis society expects of its citizens. As we saw in Chapter 3, individuals should be discreet about their desires; show reticence about sex; be in control of their passions; and be reasonable, responsible, and sensible in all aspects of daily life. By disregarding these ideals, calabai often provoke negative perceptions.

Islam and Anti-Calabai Sentiment

Islam exhorts Muslims to control their passions and be discreet in all matters pertaining to sexual activity. Of course, this is not always the reality; in same-sex groups, people can be quite explicit about sexual matters. Islam, though, offers a more powerful source of condemnation of calabai subjectivity than proclivity to broadcast sexual affairs. Islam is cited by some people as the basis for the idea that same-sex sexual relations are sinful (*dosa*).

Pak Bata', who works as a driver between Sengkang and Makassar, said that even though calabai have been given a certain fate, sexual relations between two males is still a sin and should be avoided. While Pak Bata' has calabai friends, he thinks what they do is *musyrik*, a term that literally means "polytheistic" and in this case is used to imply something sinful.

Some people believe calabai are not sincere toward Islam and that they make the pilgrimage to Mecca not for religious reasons but for self-promotion and for the status it brings. A strict Muslim man named Haji Ismail told me that calabai who go to Mecca are disgusting. Although they may apply to go to Mecca sincerely and it is hoped they will become enlightened about same-sex relationships being a sin, Haji Ismail confided that many calabai go to Mecca just to have sex; in Haji Ismail's thinking, there are many men in Mecca, and calabai thus go there to have sex with men. Such individuals will all go straight to Hell, Haji Ismail said.

Andi Zainuddin, who works at the Department of Religion in Sengkang, told me that calabai just go on the hajj so they can get the title of Haji. Then when they come home from the Holy Land (*Tanah Suci*), they continue to wear dresses. They get on the plane in trousers, Andi Zainnudin said, because otherwise they are not allowed to go to Mecca, but when they come home, they get off the plane in a dress.

Even some calabai have difficulty reconciling the incongruence between their religion and their behavior. Haji Yamin, an elderly calabai who is also a bissu, confessed s/he has a type of illness (*penyakit*). Haji Yamin is unable to fall asleep unless s/he is sleeping next to a man, but s/he knows that since s/he is a Haji, same-sex sexual relations are sinful. So when Haji Yamin is in bed, s/he lets hir toes touch the toes of the man next to hir but that is all that s/he will allow to happen.

Many calabai struggle with their desires and their religion. Some calabai are so troubled that they force themselves to change. When Haji Baco' came back from Mecca, s/he stopped dressing like a woman and refused to become involved in any romantic relationships with men. But even though s/he dressed like a man and did not have any boyfriends, s/he admits that s/he can never be completely like a man because Allah has given hir a different fate from everybody else. So what is not expressly forbidden in Islam s/he continues to do, for instance cooking, sewing, and arranging weddings.

Sometimes sexual desire and the urge to be like a woman decrease for calabai as they get older. Andi Lutfi, a 28-year-old man, told me that when they are young, calabai might think they are calabai, but as they get older they realize that, for better or worse, Allah has made them male. As such, some calabai believe that to get into heaven, they must behave according to Islamic codes of masculinity, which I outlined in Chapter 3. So older calabai often pray frequently, Andi Lutfi said, and they acknowledge their male self (*diri laki-laki*). Indeed, almost all young calabai have a woman's name, but often older calabai do not.

In the 1950s, there were a series of regional rebellions and Islam was used to justify violence against calabai; many calabai were killed. There have been more recent hostilities, too, leveled against calabai and calabai organizations. While I was in South Sulawesi in 2001, the headquarters of the Makassar gay organization, GAYa Celebes, was burned down by fundamentalist Muslims. There are then many negative views expressed about calabai.

Tolerance and Acceptance from within Islam

From reading the previous sections, it would be easy to assume that calabai are made to feel unwelcome in Bugis society. But everyday attitudes toward calabai are quite different from official discourses and also from isolated statements made by certain people. Not many people actually openly express negative opinions of calabai. I did of course wonder whether people were just offering me a positive view of calabai in an attempt to be considered enlightened and humane or because they thought that was what I wanted to hear. There may be some element of truth in this, but after a year one would tend to get a sense of general feeling toward a group.

Having heard many positive remarks about calabai being accepted in Bugis society, I wanted to make sure I received a balanced view. A visit to the Department of Religion in Sengkang seemed essential. If anyone was going to have negative views of calabai, it would be here, or so I thought.

One morning I waited by the main road for a passing horse cart (*dokar*) and asked the driver to take me to the Department of Religion. I planned to ask how many calabai go on the hajj to Mecca and how many calabai Haji there were in Sengkang. While these were not meant to be emotive questions, I thought they would encourage a discussion of views on calabai.

When I arrived at the Department, I went into the lobby and was soon joined by nine men and three women who immediately began bombarding me with all the usual questions: Where are you from? How old are you? Are you married? No? Do you want a Bugis husband? It was quite an intimidating place, as the lobby was large and open and there were a lot of new faces. Some of the women were wearing *jilbab* (head veil), and I was sure anything to do with calabai would be a taboo topic. I was hoping to be invited into a small office where someone would be duly appointed to answer my questions, but as time went on this seemed less and less likely. So eventually, I told the assembled people that I was doing research on calabai. No one looked embarrassed by my raising this topic, nor did anyone leave the room. I then ventured to ask how many calabai make the hajj to Mecca. I was told by one man, in a seemingly boastful manner, that Sengkang has more calabai who make the hajj than any other district in South Sulawesi. The man said that in 1998 there was one *kloter* of calabai who went to Mecca. *Kloter* is the acronym of Kelompok Terbang, which means Flying Group, and so this meant that one planeload of calabai went to Mecca. In 2000, only thirty calabai went on the pilgrimage, though.

While the people at the Department did joke around—for instance, one man asked me if I wanted to know what type of *alat-alat* (devices, i.e., sex toys) calabai use—there was acceptance of calabai going on the hajj and even pride that Wajo' regency had so many calabai wealthy enough to go to Mecca. To go on the hajj costs around Rp22 million (US$2,200); a civil servant earns around Rp6 million a year. What was less accepted by people was the perceived insincerity of some calabai who make the pilgrimage.

Calabai who go to on the hajj must go dressed as men. I was told, though, that many calabai confess they are very religious before they go to Mecca, but as soon as they arrive back in Sengkang they revert to their old calabai ways and wear dresses and form intimate relationships with men again. One example was shared about a calabai named Haji Yadi. Every year Haji Yadi goes on the hajj, and every year s/he makes an oath (*sumpah*) to start acting like a man. But every year, Haji Yadi comes back dressed as a woman. After this example was given, people started talking about how, for better or for worse, calabai will always be calabai, and the will of Allah was used to justify calabai subjectivity and to sanction calabai behavior.

For many Bugis, gender identity is considered something beyond an individual's control; hence, individuals cannot be held entirely responsible for their behavior. For instance, Allah determines people's fate, so whomever people become is due to Allah's omnipotence. Puang Sulai told me that calabai cannot deny (*mengingkari*) their fate (*kodrat*). Calabai have their own nature, he revealed, so no one can prohibit (*melarang*) their behavior. A man named Andi Jafri told me that there is no reason for calabai to feel shame (*malu*) about their identity because it is Allah's will that they be like this. Other people talked of calabai having a contemptible curse (*hina kutuk*) given to them by Allah that they must patiently endure (*sabar menderita*). Because Allah made people calabai, society must accept them.

The Qur'an, and various interpretations of its passages, is sometimes used to justify calabai identity. For instance, a calabai named Fatilah told me that while s/he acknowledges that the Qur'an forbids (*haram*) sexual affairs between two men, s/he stresses that relationships between calabai and their partners are not between two men, but rather they are between two different types of people (in effect, a heterogender relationship) and hence not a sin.

Specific tenets from the Qur'an are used by some calabai to affirm their subjectivity. The phrase *"Al Hunza Bil Hunza"* is interpreted by Haji Yamin to mean, "Whatever people may be, if they are true to themselves, they are not committing a sin." Haji Yamin uses this phrase to reaffirm hir identity; s/he is being true to hirself, so therefore s/he is not committing a sin in the eyes of Allah. I asked a strict Muslim man, named Haji Ismail, what he thought this phrase meant. He said that *"Al Hunza Bil Hunza"* implies that it is acceptable for a male to act like a woman and for a male to do certain things, like cooking, that women usually do. But Haji Ismail said that *"Al Hunza Bil Hunza"* does not condone homosexual behavior. There are then differing interpretations of Islam, and these interpretations can be used to both justify and condemn calabai subjectivity.

Government Support for Calabai

Perhaps surprisingly, there is support for calabai within government realms. Even some government officials in high places publicly defend the position of calabai.

Calabai in Sengkang have established their own official (*resmi*) organization called Persatuan Waria (Association of Waria). This organization is endorsed by the local government, and calabai are rightly proud of this fact. One member, named Tofi, told me that Persatuan Waria is the most famous calabai organization in all of South Sulawesi precisely because it is officially supported and funded by the local government.

One day I attended the election of the new president (*ketua*) of Persatuan Waria. I remember arriving at the hall where the election was taking place and seeing Eka across the room. Eka then signaled for me to go over to hir. When I first arrived in Indonesia, I was terribly confused by the sign for beckoning someone. The signal is made by holding the hand palm down, continually flagging the fingers in a downwards manner—I was used to people beckoning me in exactly the opposite way, with palm up and fingers repeatedly drawn upwards toward the body. When I first saw this sign, I thought people were trying to shoo me away. As you can imagine, this was not a good signal to misinterpret, as I would saunter away from the very people calling me. But when Eka signaled to me, I knew s/he was beckoning me.

Initially, there were eight candidates in the running for the presidency, but five pulled out, Eka said. Once the voting was complete—120 calabai voted—and the new president was announced, it was then time for speeches. Eka took the microphone and talked a little about the welcomed support calabai receive from the general public in Sengkang; in particular s/he emphasized that Persatuan Waria is supported and funded by the Regent's (Bupati) office. Eka thanked the District Secretary (who is referred to as Pak Sekwilda) and the other officials for overseeing the voting process and then invited Pak Sekwilda to come and say a few words.

Up to this point I had been sitting in the audience, but as Pak Sekwilda took the microphone he spied me and said, "Serli [Sharyn], Serli, come up here with me." Feeling I could not refuse, I hesitantly went up. Pak Sekwilda then put his arm around me and said into the microphone, "This here is Serli, and she is doing research on calabai, so help her out in any way you can. Invite her to your village so she can see how calabai live." Pak Sekwilda then asked me to say a few words in Bugis, which I did and everyone found it very funny—the anthropologist as clown had particular resonance at this moment. Pak Sekwilda then thanked me and indicated that I should sit on the stage with the other officials.

Pak Sekwilda started by telling the audience that they have the support of the Bupati's office. He then said that the Bupati's office would help develop the arts to keep **adat** (traditional culture) alive and that it would donate funding and facilities so that *waria* from Sengkang can beat *waria* from Sidrap at the next *adat* festival. This time Pak Sekwilda used the national Indonesian term *waria* instead of the local term *calabai*. In his comments, Pak Sekwilda noted that *waria* from the province of Sidrap had recently beat *waria* from Wajo' in a cultural competition involving dancing and singing. This hit a sore point with calabai present, and they applauded loudly when Pak Sekwilda assured them that they would defeat *waria* from Sidrap the next time. Pak Sekwilda continued by saying that we need *waria* because how could we organize weddings without *waria*? He then told the audience to make sure they did not do drugs or catch AIDS because he wanted *waria* to live a long time and prosper. Pak Sekwilda picked up here on negative aspects sometimes associated with *waria* in metropolitan areas like Jakarta, but not yet with individuals in Sengkang.

Pak Sekwilda then told the audience that it is a sin for Muslims to watch films that show fellatio (*sepong*). Pak Sekwilda added that fellatio can give you a disease that will spread all around your mouth and that fellatio and other types of sexual activity cause AIDS and PMS (*penyakit menular seksual*, "sexually transmitted infections"). At Karebosi, the central square in the capital city of Makassar, Pak Sekwilda noted that *waria* sell themselves for Rp20,000 (US$2) and he exhorted Sengkang *waria* not to involve themselves in such activities. Pak Sekwilda then drew on this knowledge of safer sex practices and stated that it is safer never to have sex or just to masturbate (**coli-coli**), but if people must engage in sexual activity, he pleaded with them to use a condom.

At this point, a person came on stage with an overhead projector, and Pak Sekwilda bent down to place the first transparency on it. I could not see the projected image from the stage, so I excused myself and gratefully returned to my seat in the audience. Gruesome images of genitalia badly inflicted with sexually transmitted infections were shown. When he got to the last transparency, Pak Sekwilda looked up and scanned the room; he then implored *waria* not to have sex but rather to just masturbate (*coli-coli aja dong*). Everyone started laughing at this comment, and Pak Sekwilda continued by saying that all of the diseases shown on the transparencies can be transmitted by the anus (*lubang dubur*), mouth, and toothbrush. Pak Sekwilda added that indeed *waria* would not be *waria* if they did not like men, but they have to be careful (*memang, bukan waria kalau tidak suka laki-laki tapi harus hati-hati*). Do not destroy the character of *waria*, Pak Sekwilda warned; if one thing is changed, then all are adversely affected (*jangan merusak citra waria, satu yang berubah dikena semua*). Pak Sekwilda's speech was met with great applause, and the audience then jostled their way onto the stage to shake hands with Pak Sekwilda and the rest of the officials.

The level of support offered by the District Secretary and other important government officials to calabai took me by surprise. There was support not just for calabai subjectivity but also for calabai activities; outperforming calabai from the province of Sidrap was a matter of town pride for the District Secretary. Employees at the Department of Religion also acknowledged calabai and the integral role they play within Bugis society, and this was something I did not expect to find.

Why This Tolerance for Calabai?

From my observations and experiences, there is in general a high degree of tolerance, and even acceptance and support, of calabai identity in Bugis South Sulawesi. What accounts for this degree of tolerance? One reason may be found in indigenous understandings of gender. As we saw in Chapter 2, gender in Bugis South Sulawesi is considered to be constituted by a number of factors; this allows acknowledgment of diverse gender subjectivities. Bugis history celebrates a multitude of gendered identities. History tells us of female warriors and gender-transcendent bissu shamans (the latter are discussed in Chapter 6), and this contributes to tolerance of gender diversity. Calabai have a recognized role in Bugis society as Wedding Mothers (*Indo' Botting*), which is explored in Chapter 7. Having a particular social function lets calabai claim a respected place in society. The aesthetic and exhibitionary skills of calabai, as displayed in cultural festivals, bring pride to regional centers when they win competitions. There is also currently a resurgence of *adat* traditional customs, and calabai are often at the forefront of cultural assertion claims.

Disparaging comments are made about calabai, particularly at official levels. In some respects, calabai identity is marginalized, and they may be teased and encouraged to be men. However, there is quite a wide support base for calabai, particularly in practical and day-to-day views of calabai, which this chapter has revealed.

CONCLUSION

This chapter has looked at ways in which calabai develop and express their sense of self. In many cases, calabai structure their identity on a mix of Bugis and Western models of femininity. As such, many calabai desire to refashion their bodies into a more feminine form. Moreover, many calabai replicate heteronormative relationships by becoming like a wife and being the receptive partner in sexual relations. In other ways, though, calabai deviate from norms of Bugis woman-hood. For instance, calabai assume economic control in romantic relationships, dress in ways inappropriate for Bugis women, socialize with men, and are often sexually explicit. In this respect, calabai thus assert an identity that differs from Bugis women and from Bugis men.

Negative sentiments are expressed with regard to calabai, and most of these stem from interpretations of Islam and from the belief that calabai cannot control their passions. Issues of social status and *siri'* also influence opinions of calabai. For instance, we saw that Yulia's high-status family was deeply shamed when Yulia refused to marry a woman; indeed, Yulia's family then left Sengkang. Many views of calabai are not negative, however. On the contrary, there is acknowledgment that calabai occupy a recognized position within Bugis society. For instance, institutions such as the Department of Religion and local government are often publicly supportive of calabai.

What comes through in this chapter is that calabai assert and occupy a distinct gendered place in Bugis society. By offering an ethnographic perspective of calabai subjectivity, we see the dynamic contribution they make to the Bugis gender system.

6

Androgynous Shamans

A BISSU CEREMONY: A PRELUDE

La Tenri Olli'
Aseng tongeng-tongeng
Mu ri langié
Mu nonno' ri lino
Mu riyaseng tédong

La Tenri Olli'
Your truest name
Up in the sky
Descend to earth
In the name of the buffalo

*This is how Mariani began her chant. The chant had an eerie tone, and it was recited to the accompaniment of a cylindrical drum (***tumba,*** B), symbols (***kancing,*** B), bamboo rattle (***lae-lae,*** B) and metal rhythm sticks (***ana' baccing,*** B). The chant signaled the start of a bissu ceremony—the instruments were to awaken the deities (***dewata***).*

*Earlier in the day, thirty-five of us had squeezed into one of two small minivans (pētē-pētē) and traveled for over an hour to reach a sacred cave. It was there that the ceremony was to be performed for Ibu Qadri. Ibu Qadri wanted to make the pilgrimage to Mecca, and s/he was seeking a blessing (***passili,*** B) from the spirit world. The only individuals able to contact the spirit world and conduct the blessing were bissu.*

*"Bismillahirrahmanirrahim"—Mariani called to Allah before climbing into a small temple (***panggung,*** B). This was one of the first bissu ceremonies I had attended, and I was somewhat baffled as to why a pious Muslim would seek a blessing from dewata to go to Mecca. Mariani explained, however, that there really is no contradiction because, while Allah is the one and only God, Allah has helpers called dewata. It is to these dewata that Mariani calls. Unwrapping a frail book, reputed to be 700 years old, Mariani began to chant again and at the same time passed the book through incense smoke:*

I am calling you, Panru Paēngnga, the one who is neither man nor woman. And it is I who am calling you because I too am neither man nor woman. Olawele' lawelo' lawelenreng . . . Oh Great Spirit, I ask you to enter the body, you who has no sex, but has a title (*gelar*).

FIGURE 6.1 Offerings for a bissu ceremony

When Mariani was in contact with the most powerful dewata, *that* dewata *arranged for the most appropriate lesser* dewata *to descend and possess* (menyurupi) *hir. Mariani was then covered with a white sheet, under which s/he tossed violently. When the sheet was removed, Mariani sat up, but Mariani's spirit was no longer there; hir body had been taken over by a* dewata. *Now possessed, Mariani revealed in the sacred bissu language that for the blessing to be a success, three other bissu must accompany hir into the cave. I was allowed to follow. After sliding down the entry passage and walking quite a distance, avoiding stepping on any scorpions, we entered a large cavern where we squatted in a circle. Mariani began to chant and, at appropriate times, the other bissu joined in.*

During our time in the cave, arrangements had been made for the main ceremony. Upon our return, Mariani took hir place in front of a large variety of ritual offerings **(sesaji),** *which included sticky rice* **(songkolo',** B) *dyed in four different colors* (sokko' patanrupa, B), *eggs, cigarettes, bananas, coconuts, a hen, and a rooster (Figure 6.1). Mariani chanted again, but this time hir chanting became frighteningly erratic. Hir body began to shake and s/he became very angry. "Where are the* **sirih** *(betel) leaves?" s/he demanded.*

Sirih *leaves were an essential part of the ceremony, and while there were some* sirih *leaves, there was not a sufficient amount. The* dewata *who possessed*

F I G U R E 6.2 Bissu contacting the spirit world

Mariani became incensed and would not give the blessing. It was conveyed through Mariani that we could, however, perform the ceremony at Ibu Qadri's house. When we finally arrived there, it was very late. The altar and the offerings were reconstructed in Ibu Qadri's living room, and bissu once again dressed themselves in their sacred (sakral) clothing.

Mariani, along with the other three bissu, started chanting in order to make contact with the spirit world (Figure 6.2). In order to prove that they were possessed and thus could bless Ibu Qadri's upcoming journey to Mecca, bissu performed **ma'giri'** *(B). Ma'giri' involves each bissu taking hir sword (keris) and trying to force it into hir neck (Figure 6.3), stomach (Figure 6.4), palm (Figure 6.5), or eye (Figure 6.6). If they are possessed by a powerful dewata, the keris will not penetrate their skin and they will not bleed.*

During this ritual, when Mariani completed the ma'giri', there was blood coming from hir neck. When I ventured to question this, Mariani revealed that the spirit who possessed hir was not powerful and that as a result s/he was not impenetrable **(kebal)**. *However, with the collective efforts of the other bissu, Ibu Qadri received her blessing.*

Some months later Haji Qadri successfully made the pilgrimage to Mecca. She has now returned and is requesting another bissu ceremony to give thanks to dewata for protecting her on her journey; but that's another story...

WHO ARE BISSU?

In this chapter's prelude, I recounted a bissu ceremony performed for a woman hoping to undertake the pilgrimage to Mecca. While this brief account detailed

FIGURE 6.3 Bissu performing a self-stabbing ritual (*ma'giri'*)

FIGURE 6.4 Bissu performing a self-stabbing ritual (*ma'giri'*)

FIGURE 6.5 Bissu performing a self-stabbing ritual (*ma'giri'*)

a few of the important roles of bissu—for instance, contacting the spirit world, becoming possessed, and bestowing blessings—it left untouched many other aspects of the life and roles of bissu. In this chapter I will explore in more depth bissu subjectivity and examine how individuals become bissu and what being bissu involves. I will also assess social reactions to bissu, especially those reactions that stem from an Islamic base. Inherent within all of these discussions are notions of bissu contributions to the Bugis gender system.[1]

Through the narratives of bissu, particularly Mariani, Haji Yamin, and Haji Sungke', we will see that the most important attribute bissu share is that they incorporate both female and male elements. Only an individual who embodies the energy of both male and female is powerful enough to contact the spirit world. I will explore why having female and male elements is a necessary, but not a sufficient, quality for an individual to be considered bissu. Indeed, bissu may only be recognized as embodying male and female elements after they have experienced an epiphanic dream, for example.

Bissu candidates undergo certain rites of passage before they are socially recognized as bissu, and I will look at the process of becoming bissu. I will also investigate the functions bissu perform, the events at which bissu bestow blessings, and how bissu contact the spirit world. Bugis society is strongly Islamic, but bissu traditions and rituals were around long before Islam came to Sulawesi. As such, I will also examine how bissu are socially located within a predominantly Muslim society.

What does the term *bissu* mean? Andi Galib, an educated Bugis man, told me that the term *bissu* is a Buddhist term that was taken up in South Sulawesi after the region was visited by an influential monk. Indeed, the Sanskrit word *bhiksu* is a

FIGURE 6.6 Bissu performing a self-stabbing ritual (*ma'giri'*)

term for a Buddhist monk. Bissu is a difficult word to translate into English, though. Initially I was going to use the term *priest* because if people in Indonesia explain bissu to someone who is unfamiliar with this subjectivity, they will tend to say bissu are a type of *pendeta* (religious minister). However, I have decided to use the term *shaman* because it seems to most closely approximate bissu subjectivity. Shaman is a term that describes healers and spiritual leaders. Shamans go into a trance, helped along by drums, dancing, self-harm, and deprivation. While in such a trance, shaman cross into the spiritual world to seek the information needed to bestow blessings and cure illnesses and other misfortunes. The term *shaman* seems to be compatible with the roles of *bissu*.

In referring to bissu subjectivity, I also use the term *androgynous*. Derived from the Greek *andros,* meaning male, and *gyne,* meaning female, *androgynous* is a useful term to use in reference to bissu constitution. Bissu are considered to comprise both female and male elements, but this can be a symbolic composition rather than an overt biological one. One shortcoming of using the term *androgynous* in relation to bissu is that bissu are also considered to be part deity, and the definition of *androgynous* does not take this into account.

BISSU CONSTITUTION

Mariani

It was recognized early on that Mariani had special powers and that s/he needed to be raised by someone who could help develop hir spiritual abilities. A bissu *nenek* (grandparent) was thus chosen to instruct Mariani in the ways of becoming a bissu. When s/he was still a child, Mariani therefore went to live with hir *nenek*. While hir *nenek* passed away many years ago, Mariani remembers hir fondly and carries a sacred *keris* bequeathed to hir by hir *nenek* to signal their continued connection.

To look at Mariani, you might guess that s/he is in hir 40s, but s/he is many years older than that. Indeed, there are photos of Mariani taken in hir youth, and s/he is standing alongside friends who now look comparatively old. Mariani's secret elixir is known only to hir, but s/he hints that it relates to hir bissu powers.

Mariani still lives in the same village where s/he was born. While s/he is reputedly very wealthy, s/he saves almost all of the money s/he earns from conducting blessings. Hir simple house spans two levels, although the downstairs section is cordoned into two tiny, dark flats. A family of five lives in one of the flats. The first time I stayed with Mariani, the newest arrival to their family, Fatima, had just been born. A 26-year-old man named Dani lives in the other flat. Dani makes a living from various odd jobs, and he also helps Mariani move equipment and other ritual paraphernalia. The upstairs part of the house is where Mariani lives, and it is frequently full of visitors who have traveled great distances to request blessings. Unlike the downstairs level of the house, which is made of concrete and thus stays cool, the upstairs level has corrugated iron walls and roof—corrugated iron being a sign of wealth. The ceiling is very low, less than 6 feet from the floor. The low ceiling, combined with the corrugated iron, makes the upper level incredibly hot, and I would sweat from just sitting in there. The upper level consists of a lounge room, where bissu ceremonies are performed; a bedroom; a kitchen; and an altar room. Scattered throughout the house is a large collection of ritual paraphernalia.

Bissu origins are thought to stem from the spirit world. When bissu descend to earth, they become part mortal, in addition to remaining part deity. Bissu are also regarded as predifferentiated beings. While most humans divide into either female or male beings before birth, bissu do not and thus remain a combination of both female and male. This union of female and male, mortal and deity, underpins bissu identity, and it is the reason they are considered such potent beings.

Mariani sees hirself as part deity (*dewata*) because of the connection s/he maintains with the spirit world and part human (**manusia**) because s/he lives in this world. If Mariani was merely human, s/he would not be able to contact *dewata* and conduct blessings for people. If s/he was just part of the spiritual realm, then s/he would not be able to live in this world. The combination of being both female and male means that s/he is more powerful (**sakti**) than merely an individual man or woman, neither of whom would be powerful enough to contact the spirit world nor to be possessed (**disurupi**) by *dewata*. If you cannot be possessed, then you cannot possibly be bissu. So for Mariani, it is the combination of being both female and male, and both *manusia* and *dewata,* that makes hir bissu.

How does Mariani embody male and female elements? One day when Mariani and I were talking about embodiment, s/he told me that for hir, hir right side is male. As evidence of this, s/he pointed to the whiskers that grow only on the right side of hir face. Then s/he pointed to the left side of hir face, asserting that on this side no whiskers grow. Mariani said that if s/he plucked the whiskers on hir right side, this would be a sign of rejecting hir maleness. Moreover, s/he would get ill if s/he plucked those whiskers because it would cause a disturbance within hir body. No whiskers grow on hir left side, though, because this is hir female side. Mariani also dresses in such a way as to signal ambiguity. For instance, when dressed in ritual clothing, Mariani often wears feminine symbols (e.g., flowers) on hir left side and male symbols (e.g., a *keris*) on hir right side. This understanding and representation of sexual and gender ambiguity suggests that Mariani sees hir androgynous nature in terms of a lateral division between feminine and masculine attributes.

Mariani recognizes that bissu must be ascetic (i.e., they must intensively practice self-discipline, meditation, and self-denial), but s/he confesses that for a long time s/he found it hard to constantly forsake all earthly desires. The difficulty Mariani faced meant s/he had to delay hir nomination to become **Puang Matoa,** the head of the bissu community. If a bissu is Puang Matoa, no indiscretions are tolerated. Not only must Mariani abstain from sex but s/he must not have any desires at all, and s/he is not permitted to indulge in pleasures like drinking tea or coffee or eating sugar or any type of confectionary.

Haji Yamin

Haji Yamin is a devout Muslim; s/he has made the pilgrimage to Mecca twenty-seven times. Almost without fail, Haji Yamin prays five times a day, even excusing hirself from important meetings to ensure hir prayers are made at the correct times: pre-dawn (*Subuh*), noon (*Lohor*), afternoon (*Ashar*), sunset (*Magrib*), and evening (*Isya*). Haji Yamin habitually dons the Islamic *peci* cap, which is a stark contrast to hir dark eyeliner and pink lip gloss. Haji Yamin is a bissu, and in ways like this s/he affirms the requirement of combining female and male elements.

Haji Yamin has granted hundreds of blessings in hir seventy-odd years. S/he recognizes, though, that s/he is getting older, so s/he has passed many of hir bissu duties on to hir younger apprentices (*anak buah*). Haji Yamin no longer undergoes ritual possession by *dewata,* which is an essential activity if bissu are to bestow blessings. However, Haji Yamin's expertise in all bissu rituals, traditions, and the sacred bissu language is still recognized by hir apprentices and followers.

Haji Yamin considers that the power of bissu stems from their androgynous nature. As Haji Yamin is more visibly male than female, I questioned hir one day about how s/he combines male and female elements. S/he said that bissu embody male and female by being neither solely one nor the other. For instance, Haji Yamin said that bissu should not have a penis; if they do have a penis, the penis must not live (*tidak bisa hidup kontolnya*, i.e., the penis cannot get erect). Haji Yamin then asked if I wanted proof that s/he did not have a penis. I was too stunned to answer this question immediately, and Haji Yamin took my procrastination as a yes. S/he lifted hir sarong and, with legs parted, revealed that s/he has no visible penis. S/he patted hir genitals, laughing and saying, "Here is the proof, to be a bissu you cannot have a penis." The way in which Haji Yamin interprets androgyny, essential for bissu subjectivity, is for female and male elements to be contained within one body with no distinctive features of either maleness or femaleness.

Haji Yamin told me that asceticism is also necessary for bissu to perform their social roles. To be a true bissu, individuals must refrain from any type of sexual activity and even lustful desire of any earthly thing (*tanpa nafsu*). Moreover, bissu cannot expel bodily fluids such as semen or menstrual blood. If bissu break the rules of asceticism, there are punishments. In the past, a bissu caught in wrongful sexual relations might have been killed. Punishments nowadays are not so severe, but a bissu's social status will be undermined. For instance, early on in my fieldwork, I went with a number of bissu to a large village wedding. We were all getting ready when a calabai ran upstairs and urged us to come and look for men (*mencari cowok*). I was not yet ready for the wedding, so I declined the offer, but one bissu quickly looked around for a mirror, fixed hir hair, added a little makeup, straightened hir clothes, and went downstairs with the calabai. Someone told me later that that particular bissu often looked for men at weddings, and sexual activity, such as *main karaoke* ("play karaoke," a euphemism for fellatio), frequently followed. This bissu's behavior was tolerated to an extent, but comments were still made, such as "How can s/he be bissu when s/he's behaving like that?" Such behavior undermined this individual's status as bissu.

Ascetic practices and sexual abstinence are thus creators and signifiers of potency. If a being embodies male and female aspects, mortal and deity elements, and forgoes all earthly desires, that individual has the foundation necessary for being bissu. But these qualities do not automatically guarantee the title of bissu. Rather, bissu candidates must undertake a long and arduous path before they are recognized as bissu.

BISSU RITES OF PASSAGE

If an individual has the foundation to be a bissu, that person may receive the calling to become a bissu. This calling comes in different forms. Haji Yamin was born intersexed and so had physical evidence that s/he was destined to be bissu. Mariani received the calling through an epiphanic dream; this is how it is for many bissu, including Haji Sungke'.

Haji Sungke'

Haji Sungke' has been a bissu for a great many years. I never asked hir age, but s/he appears quite old. Haji Sungke' lives in a tiny village on the northeast coast of South Sulawesi. S/he has a lovely home with spacious rooms filled to bursting with the most intriguing bissu paraphernalia. Haji Sungke' claims hir social status not just through being bissu; s/he wears many other hats. Haji Sungke' is a ritual dance expert, and s/he is the person bissu refer to when deciding which ritual dance to do and the correct way to perform it. S/he not only teaches other bissu traditional dances but also holds classes for local children. One time I was watching Haji Sungke' show a group of children a particular step used in the *pakkarēna* dance. One of the children boldly told Haji Sungke' that s/he did the step incorrectly. Haji Sungke' responded with a quirky smile, saying that s/he was just making sure that the children were paying attention.

Haji Sungke' was for a long time oblivious of the special role s/he would play in life. Then one night, without warning, s/he had a powerful dream. The dream gave hir all the knowledge (*pengetahuan*) needed to become bissu. In hir dream, s/he had a teacher whom s/he refers to as Séuwaé. S/he said the dreaming process was like being semiconscious, where s/he was neither awake nor asleep. First, Haji Sungke' dreamed in Javanese, but s/he did not accept the instructions on being bissu in this language and so the dream came again in the Makassar language, which s/he also refused. Finally, the dream came in Bugis and s/he was happy with this. Haji Sungke' then studied for eight days and eight nights through hir dreams on how to be bissu. The dreams taught hir the sacred bissu language. The notion of epiphanic dreams is not uncommon, and a dream that persuades an individual to become bissu signals the start of a long process.

Mariani on Becoming Bissu

Individuals should be aware of their **bakat** (talent) to be bissu by their early teens, Mariani told me. At this age, if not earlier, bissu candidates go to a special place, such as a house where many bissu live, where they learn about being bissu. Importantly, though, Mariani said that bissu are not taught the sacred bissu language; if a candidate does not already know the language (e.g., if s/he has not been taught this language through a dream), then s/he is not true bissu. It is essential for bissu candidates to have a real desire (*punya keinginan kuat*) to become bissu because the training is long and hard. Candidates must be rigorous in their study of the sacred bissu instruments and how to use them. They must learn and memorize numerous *mantra*. Candidates are required to study and understand the knowledge and the magic associated with being bissu. Bissu candidates must also learn the ritual dances, the chants, and the proper way of arranging offerings. They must also learn all the various rituals and ritual prayers. Candidates must also learn lengthy genealogies (*silsilah*) and develop an understanding of the sacred texts. Bissu candidates must be able to act as a home for spirits called to earth, heal the sick, and bestow blessings. Once bissu candidates, who are referred to as bissu **mamata** (B, "unripe" bissu) can do all this, Mariani told me that they become bissu **tanré** (B, "high" bissu).

Before bissu *mamata* are promoted to bissu *tanré,* there is a final rite of passage they must undergo. According to Mariani, this rite of passage takes place over three days and three nights. During this period, the bissu *mamata* is in a state of semiconsciousness (*direbba*), which is described as like almost being dead. The bissu *mamata* is wrapped in white taffeta cloth (*kain kafan*) and placed on a wooden raft. The raft is then launched into a river—a variation of this rite of passage is performed in Luwu regency where a bissu *mamata* must sleep beneath a royal umbrella (*payung tompo'tikka,* B). After the three nights, the bissu *tanré* emerges (*muncul*), and s/he is bathed in the river and ordained (*dilantik*) as a bissu.

During this final rite of passage, Mariani said that the spirit of the bissu rises to the heavens. While there, the bissu spirit asks for permission from *dewata* to become a bissu *tanré*. Only a real bissu, who embodies both male and female and mortal and deity elements, is able to make this journey. If the bissu candidate is really a man, for instance, he will not be able to contact the spirit world. When I questioned why it was necessary for bissu to embody both male and female elements, Mariani said that we do not know if God is male or female, so only someone who is both male and female can mediate with the spirit world and be possessed (*kadongkokang,* B). So what happens when a bissu *mamata* acquires all the relevant knowledge and receives permission from the spirit world to become a bissu *tanre*? What does life involve for bissu?

BISSU LIFE

Mariani, Haji Yamin, and Haji Sungke' all successfully passed through the initiation rituals and became bissu *tanré*. As fully fledged bissu, numerous expectations are placed on Mariani, Haji Yamin, and Haji Sungke', and they perform many roles in Bugis society.

Bugis mythology abounds with legends of bissu and the roles they played in the past. Bissu are said to have made the world blossom and to have first brought life to earth. Indeed, bissu are often believed to have facilitated the first earthly marriage. Tales are told of bissu guarding the sacred regalia and of organizing and protecting the royal courts. Bissu continue to perform many of these functions today. As we will see in Chapter 7, bissu still play a vital role in some Bugis weddings. However, the role of bissu and their position in Bugis society changed dramatically in the mid-twentieth century.

Until 1957, South Sulawesi was politically divided into noble-dominated kingdoms, which held political and social power. In 1957, however, these kingdoms began to be rapidly replaced by a centralized national government. The disbandment of the kingdoms severely undermined the position of bissu, who had previously defined their social role around the royal courts. During this period, the influence of the overtly Islamic Kahar Muzakkar movement began to grow. This movement sought to suppress local cultural practices, which of course included bissu activities. From the late 1950s, bissu rituals had to be conducted covertly, if they could be conducted at all.

For almost half a century, bissu activities were officially outlawed. In 1998, however, there was a dramatic change in Indonesian politics. President Suharto's New Order government lost power, and in its wake came moves to revitalize

FIGURE 6.7 A woman requesting a bissu blessing for good health

traditional cultural practices. As a way of asserting ethnic identity, bissu were embraced as a unique and fascinating part of Bugis culture.

I first went to Sulawesi in 1998, and since then I have witnessed the increasing popularity of bissu rituals. In 2000, a number of bissu from South Sulawesi were invited to go to Bali and Java to perform at cultural festivals. In 2001, I was selected to participate in a National Geographic series on PhD candidates conducting interesting research; bissu were the focus of this documentary (Tomaszewski et al., 2001). In September 2002, a small group of bissu traveled to Japan to participate in an international traditional culture festival. Also in 2002, foreign academics and the Governor of South Sulawesi were officially welcomed to the International La Galigo Conference by bissu. Bissu have inspired two stage plays, *The Language of the Gods* by Louis Nowra (1999) and Robert Wilson's production *I La Galigo* (2004). If bissu activities were limited to these arenas, it could be argued that bissu and bissu rituals have merely become art. But as we will see, bissu still have immense cultural importance and utility. So what functions do bissu undertake in contemporary Bugis society?

The most important role of bissu is to grant blessings. Bissu bestow blessings in order to ensure good harvests (*mappalilli'*, B) and to protect society against natural disasters (*bencana alam*) such as floods, cyclones, storms, and droughts. In order to avoid a natural disaster, bissu perform what is called the *maccera' wanua* (B) ceremony. Bissu bless people before they undertake a journey, and they conduct blessings to heal the sick (Figures 6.7 and 6.8). Bissu also officiate at life-cycle rituals, such as births, deaths, and marriages.

FIGURE 6.8 A woman requesting a bissu blessing for a safe journey

In many ways, bissu have the freedom to practice the customs that they enjoyed before the 1950s, and in this sense there is continuity of culture. One significant change, though, is that while bissu ceremonies were previously only conducted for the nobility, now in the era of reformation (*era reformasi*) ordinary people can and do request bissu blessings. What defines the people who request bissu blessings is not their wealth or lineage but their strong belief in the power of bissu.

One of the blessings I frequently heard requested was for a safe pilgrimage to Mecca, like the one I recounted at the start of this chapter. But any journey is worthy of receiving a blessing. East Timor's protracted struggle for independence came to a head during my main fieldwork period, and many people requested blessings for the safe return of Bugis relatives living there.

Blessings are also performed to cure people of particular illnesses. Mariani receives visitors almost every day requesting blessings to cure an illness. Bissu then call on the spirit world and invite *dewata* to tell them what medicine (*mujangka*, B) is needed, and how to make it. Often the *mujangka* given to them is in the form of water taken from a sacred well. Curing the sick sometimes provides proof for nonbelievers of the power of bissu. Pak Paha told me that he never believed in bissu magic until he was given *mujangka* and then a miracle (*ajaib*) caused him to get better. For others, the proof is in the fact that people remain ill if they do not go to bissu.

Bissu also perform fertility blessings and help with pregnancies. Haji Sungke', whom we met before, is a bissu, and s/he also practices as a midwife (in Indonesian a term for midwife is **dukun beranak,** and while the term does not have gender connotations, like it does in English, most *dukun beranak* are women). On the front door of the house belonging to Haji Sungke' is a large sign saying, "Haji Sungke', Dukun Beranak." In hir house there are many altars (*lamolong,* B), and it is in front of these that blessings are performed for newborn babies. Haji Sungke' relies on hir connection with the spirit world to ensure that babies are born physically and mentally perfect (*sempurna*). The relationship between Haji Sungke' and the mother-to-be starts when the woman first finds out that she is pregnant. If the woman has any problems, Haji Sungke' often has the skills to rectify these. For instance, Haji Sungke' is able to turn around a baby in the womb if the baby is breech. When the woman's water breaks, Haji Sungke' is called and helps deliver the baby. When s/he was younger, s/he used to do it on hir own, but now Haji Sungke' works in collaboration with the local health clinic (*puskesmas*). Being part of the local health clinic brings a level of legitimacy to hir role, and s/he proudly displays the black doctor's bag s/he was given, on the side of which is written "Dukun Kit, Puskesmas."

Bissu also play a role in circumcision (**sunat**) ceremonies. Almost all Muslim boys in Indonesia are circumcised, generally between the ages of 6 and 12, although some boys may be as old as 15 or as young as a few months. Male circumcision is a public affair and elaborately celebrated. In South Sulawesi, Muslim girls too are commonly circumcised, although the women I talked to described their circumcision, which generally took place sometime between the ages of 5 and 9, as a symbolic ritual.

I remember one particular circumcision of a girl where Mariani performed the main blessing. Mariani took care of the general organization of the ceremony and instructed people how to do certain things. The night before the circumcision took place there was a prayer reading (*barasanji*) where songs were sung in praise of Muhammad. Mariani arranged all of the ritual food, including *ka'do' minynya'* (B), which is a rice mixture with an egg placed on top. The next morning the girl was dressed in *baju bodo* (a traditional Bugis blouse), and a female *dukun* (traditional medical practitioner) took a small, clean hen and encouraged the hen to peck the girl's clitoris. The *dukun* and Mariani recited a number of ritual blessings and then the procedure was over.

Bissu bless construction sites and perform house consecrations, the latter being alternatively referred to as *maccēra' bola* (B) and *massalama' bola* (B). Bissu bless the general process of construction, and people seek information from bissu as to the best date to start building. Dani, the man who lives below Mariani, told me that in 1977 a company wanted to start a new quarry and, because the company knew it was important for the local people, a bissu blessing was commissioned. To ensure that the construction process was given an extra powerful blessing, a buffalo was slaughtered. The morning after the blessing, however, the slaughtered buffalo's head turned into a woman's head, and the bissu who had performed the blessing were accused of murder. As punishment, the bissu were banished from their homeland for six years. When the bissu finally returned home, the six men who had sentenced them were found dead within twenty-four hours. This story serves to show the darker side of bissu power.

Bissu also bless agricultural events, and one of the most important blessings is the harvest festival, called *mappalilli* (B). Before harvesting begins, bissu contact the spirit world and seek permission to remove the sacred plough (*bajak*), which is inhabited by *dewata,* from its resting place at the *Bola Ridié* (B, yellow house). The plough is then taken to the fields so that *dewata* can bestow a blessing. It is crucial that bissu do not pretend to be possessed by spirits and just give permission for the plough to be removed because this would result in catastrophe; at the very least, crops would fail. So bissu must prove they are possessed before giving any blessings. But how do bissu prove possession?

PROVING POSSESSION

Bau Muliyardi, a high-ranking Bugis man, told me that the process of proving possession varies according to the area where bissu live. In Soppeng district, for instance, bissu walk through fire. If bissu manage to do this without getting burned, this proves they have been entered by a powerful spirit (*disurupi*). Other bissu walk over hot coals in bare feet. If bissu complete this task without getting hurt, it confirms that the spirits are protecting them. Some bissu swallow blades, and if they do so without cutting themselves, they are deemed inhabited by *dewata*. Perhaps the most renowned way of verifying possession, though, is by performing *ma'giri'* (B).

As noted previously, *ma'giri'* is a dramatic ritual, and its spectacular nature ensures bissu ceremonies are especially exciting to watch. When National Geographic was making their documentary on my fieldwork, they made sure they recorded bissu performing *ma'giri'*. One particularly impressive performance I saw occurred when an entire village came together to request a blessing for their rice fields. This blessing involved six bissu, one of whom was Mariani.

Along with the other bissu, Mariani and I arrived at the small village early one morning and were directed to the home of one of the village elders. As soon as we were inside the house, bissu started setting up their paraphernalia, making particular decorations and getting the offerings ready (Figure 6.9). This took most of the day, and it was not until evening that bissu announced that the ceremony could begin. After bissu finished getting dressed in their sacred costumes (Figure 6.10), they gathered together and started chanting and burning incense. To the side of the bissu sat a small group of drummers who gradually began beating louder and quicker; the chanters followed suit. The chanting was performed to entice *dewata* to descend to earth and possess the bissu. As the *dewata* possessed the bissu, the behavior of the bissu became erratic. When the bissu were possessed, they stood up and in a circle danced around the room to the beat of the drums. Then the bissu formed pairs, and one bissu fell backwards, supported by the other bissu who was standing on hir partner's foot. Next, the bissu all took out their *keris* and began forcing them into various parts of the body, for instance, eyes, necks, temples, stomachs, and palms. If bissu were possessed by potent *dewata*, the *keris* would not penetrate their skin. Mariani once told me that some bissu have actually died because they were not impenetrable (*kebal*). After about five minutes, the drumming stopped; so too did the bissu.

FIGURE 6.9 Bissu making offerings for an upcoming blessing ceremony

FIGURE 6.10 Bissu in their sacred clothing

Having proved they were possessed, bissu could perform the blessing of the village crops. The bissu sat in a semicircle facing about 100 people who had precariously squeezed into the wooden stilt house. Through the bissu, *dewata* said that the gifts prepared for their propitiation were adequate and, as such, the village would have a successful harvest. With the blessing performed, *dewata* were returned to the spirit world in a final ceremony to "lay down the sword" (*makkangulu telle makna benno na tudang ata wa bekkeng,* B).

As we can see, bissu play many significant roles in Bugis society. Bissu ensure safe travel, heal the sick, grant fertility blessings, facilitate circumcision ceremonies, give consent for construction work to begin, and ensure agricultural success. Bissu are able to perform such blessings because they are a powerful combination of female and male attributes and mortal and deity elements. There have been many changes to the role and position of bissu in the last century, but bissu rituals have never died out, and indeed today there is almost a bissu renaissance. But how does Bugis society view bissu, especially since most people in Bugis South Sulawesi adhere to Islam?

BEING BISSU IN A MUSLIM SOCIETY

Bugis are often cited as among the most Islamic of all peoples in Indonesia. But devotion to Islam does not necessarily preclude the practice of Bugis traditions or adherence to indigenous belief systems, as the practices of bissu and the current popularity of bissu rituals affirm. So how do bissu fit into a Muslim society?

Anti-Bissu Sentiment

The relationship between bissu and Islam has often been a volatile one. During the 1950s and 1960s, Islam was cited by some people as the basis for deeming bissu identity and rituals as sinful. Some bissu were violently persecuted by fundamentalist Muslims. For instance, some bissu were forced to shave their heads to publicly signify their supposed immorality. Haji Mappaganti told me that many bissu were tortured, and some were even murdered. During this time, Mariani and some other surviving bissu were forced to retreat to the hills to avoid persecution. In the 1960s, an Islamic militia group called Ansor killed many bissu. The Kahar Muzakkar movement also considered bissu to be sinful according to Islam, and they forcibly stopped bissu activities and burned or threw into the ocean their sacred instruments.

During my fieldwork, some people expressed views of bissu as sinning against Islam, and they cited parts of the Qur'an as evidence. One Islamic leader (*ulama*) told me bissu were accursed (*terkutuk*), and their practices were shameful (*aib*). A man called Pak Sultan said that Islam recognizes only one god, Allah, and the prophet Muhammad, and if anyone says anything contrary, which he believes bissu do, it is a sin (*musyrik,* literally "polytheistic").

More common than such extreme views are hints of skepticism. Andi Mansur does not believe in bissu rituals, although he thinks people have a right to believe in whatever they want. In fact, Andi Mansur admitted it would be a shame if Bugis traditions were lost completely. Puang Sulai said that he does not really believe in bissu rituals, but he is too afraid not to believe at all. So Puang Sulai believes just enough so that if the link bissu claim to have with the spirit world is real, he will still be rewarded in the afterlife. But his belief has a limit; as a Muslim, Puang Sulai prays only to Allah, not to any pre-Islamic deities.

In Bugis society, there is skepticism about bissu practices, and at times there has even been persecution of bissu. But in many ways, a more interesting phenomenon is the coexistence of Islam and bissu traditions and the Muslim justification for seeking a bissu blessing to ensure a safe pilgrimage to Mecca.

Coexistence

One reason why bissu practices manage to coexist with Islam is the current national emphasis on advocating local traditions. Bissu are now promoted by people in local and national governments as a distinctive aspect of Bugis traditional culture (*adat*), and *adat* is considered quite separate from religion (**agama**). This separation means that bissu practices are not seen as undermining or competing against Islam. In a way, bissu practices survive because they are seen as a part of *adat,* not a part of *agama.* Indeed, there is a saying in South Sulawesi that goes, "Makassar people hold tight to religion. Bugis people hold tight to *adat* (*Orang Makassar kuat agama. Orang Bugis kuat adat*)." This saying indicates the importance many Bugis place on culture.

Perhaps a more powerful reason why bissu practices can coexist with Islam is that the latter is able to accommodate other belief structures. Andi Galib, an elderly Bugis man, told me that when Islamic traders first came to Sulawesi, they believed in God (*Tuhan*), just like the people of Sulawesi. But the traders called their god "Allah," while Andi Galib's ancestors called their god "Patoto'ē." Eventually, Andi Galib said, people in Sulawesi also began calling Patoto'ē, Allah. Similarly, Haji Yamin, who is a bissu, said that pre-Islamic Bugis gods and Allah are all the same; they are just called different names because of cultural adaptations. Haji Yamin used the example of cars. Long ago, he said, we did not believe in cars, but now we do because our belief system has changed. Because our belief system continually adapts, Haji Yamin maintains that we can believe in bissu practices and incorporate them into an Islamic structure. In this way, past belief systems are legitimized in a contemporary setting.

In some instances, what has resulted from the meeting of Islamic and bissu practices is a melding of forms of belief and custom. In the introduction to this chapter, I recounted a bissu ritual where Mariani started the blessing by using the Islamic/Arabic term *Bismillahirrahmanirrahim,* which means, "In the name of Allah, Most Gracious, Most Merciful." Mariani then proceeded to chant in the sacred bissu language, but not before seeking forgiveness from the deities (*dewata*) because s/he is a Muslim and bows before Allah, not before any *dewata.* In this way, Mariani incorporates both Islamic and bissu belief systems.

Mariani has a complex understanding of how Islam and bissu practices coexist. Mariani sees the Bugis belief structure as hierarchical. At the apex is Allah. Helping Allah are *dewata*, and *dewata* bow down before Allah. Below *dewata* are bissu, followed lower down by human beings. It is acceptable, Mariani believes, to request the help of *dewata* in contacting Allah because Allah is still acknowledged as the one true god.

In a similar way, Haji Baco' told me that d*ewata* assist Allah. Haji Baco' thinks that Allah cannot be bothered with all of humanity's tiny problems, and so Allah needs helpers. The belief system for Haji Baco' is thus structured like a parliament. Allah is the president (*presiden*) and *dewata* are the ministers. So there are ministers like the Wind Deity (*Dewa Angin*), Ocean Deity (*Dewa Laut*), and Rice Deity (*Dewi Sri*). In this way, bissu practices are sheltered under the umbrella of Islam and thus remain legitimate practice. It is important to note, though, that not all people can accommodate bissu practices into their Islamic belief structures, and for many staunch Muslims, bissu rituals continue to be considered animistic (*animisme*) and therefore sinful.

Another reason why bissu traditions have persisted is that when Islam entered Indonesia, traditional practices that were not in accordance with Islam were thrown away (*terbuang*). According to a man named Andi Sangkala, one practice that was discarded was idolatry (**keberhalaan**)—the worship of idols. Andi Sangkala acknowledges that Allah's presence is everywhere and that Allah is not just reachable in a mosque (**mesjid**). But, Andi Sangkala stresses, while Allah is everywhere, you cannot just pray anywhere. In pre-Islamic times, farmers may have prayed to a tree if they wanted a good harvest, but this was worshipping an idol, which is prohibited in Islam, and so it was stopped. Andi Mangko', an *adat* expert, said Bugis society would be ashamed (*malu*) to practice things that Islam forbids (*larang*). For instance, he told me people used to eat field mice (*tikus*), but this no longer happens because Islam forbids it. Andi Mangko' also revealed that bissu ceremonies used to involve self-immolation, but this stopped when people converted to Islam because harming oneself is explicitly forbidden. Interestingly, Mariani said that while performing *ma'giri'* is an attempt to harm yourself, it is not a sin. Mariani believes that if what s/he is doing is considered a sin by Allah, the next time s/he performs *ma'giri'* Allah will not let hir be impenetrable and s/he will die.

One visitor to Sulawesi suggested that by 1950 bissu would become mere performers, that they would turn "from priests into clowns" (Holt, 1939:35). When I asked Haji Baco' what s/he thought of the possibility of bissu fading away, s/he scoffed, telling me that bissu practices are anything but a dying tradition. In fact, there are many reasons to feel confident about the future of bissu. For instance, Mariani has just taken an aspiring bissu candidate from the village of Taraweang under hir tutelage. This village now claims genealogical records of forty generations of bissu.

As we have seen, there are a number of reasons why bissu traditions have not disappeared, even under Islamic encroachment. Bissu customs were modified or removed so that they did not explicitly go against Islam. The pre-Islamic god became known as Allah, and *dewata* became seen as Allah's assistants. Bugis history abounds in tales of powerful androgynous beings, and bissu draw on this past to legitimate their current position in society and find space for their practices within practical Islam. Indonesia is undergoing a cultural revival at present, and Bugis society has drawn upon bissu to showcase their rich cultural heritage. Haji Yamin, Haji Sungke', and Haji Baco' are all devout Muslims, they have been to Mecca, and they are bissu. There are ways, then, in which Islam and bissu can and do coexist.

CONCLUSION

I began this chapter with a fieldwork prelude recounting a bissu ceremony performed for a woman about to undertake the pilgrimage to Mecca. This prelude introduced Mariani and the roles s/he performs as bissu. Relying on ethnographic material, I then explored bissu identity. First, I examined bissu embodiment. Haji Yamin and Mariani revealed ways in which bissu constitution is understood. While their interpretations differ, Haji Yamin and Mariani both acknowledge the fundamental importance of bissu embodying female and male elements. This combination implies that bissu are predifferentiated, that is, they did not divide to become female or male beings when they were born but rather they remained a combination of both. Predifferentiation is for some people a fusion of male and female, whereas for others it is a combination in which the respective contributions remain intact, with a juxtaposition of female on the left side and male on the right side. Some bissu further achieve an androgynous persona through combining masculine and feminine symbols and clothing. Bissu predifferentiation indicates that they have maintained their connection with the spirit world, thus facilitating their contact with *dewata*.

With this understanding of bissu, I then looked at ways of becoming bissu. While bissu must embody male and female elements, such a constitution does not mean that an individual can automatically become a bissu. Rather, bissu must undergo many rites of passage. Bissu candidates must learn the sacred bissu language, be able to recite genealogies, and must gain the ability to undergo possession. The only way bissu can achieve these requirements, especially the latter, is by having a close connection with the spirit world. This connection necessitates the embodiment of male and female elements because bissu commonly believe that only predifferentiated beings have the power to connect with the spirit world.

Having completed the appropriate rites of passage, bissu take on many different roles. Some of the most important roles include bestowing blessings for an assortment of requests, such as for a successful journey or a plentiful harvest, or to cure an ailment. The main reason bissu are called on to perform such blessings is that they can mediate and communicate with the spirit world, something that is essential for the fulfillment of these blessings.

This chapter also explored how bissu are incorporated into contemporary Bugis society, which is strongly Islamic. While Islamic doctrines provide a basis and justification for anti-bissu sentiment, currently there is little overt discrimination leveled against bissu and bissu practices. I examined a number of reasons for the coexistence of Islam and bissu practices. For instance, when Islam entered the archipelago, traditional Bugis beliefs were incorporated into Islam (e.g., traditional deities became seen as Allah's helpers). Some bissu practices were also changed or abandoned in line with Islamic thinking, thus promoting a sense of convergence. The renewed interest in *adat* has also fostered an environment conducive to supporting bissu practices.

Bissu constitute an integral part of Bugis society. Not only do they provide continuity with the past but bissu continue to serve vital functions in Bugis society, such as bestowing blessings to ensure the prosperity of a community. The ability of bissu to perform such roles hinges on their capacity to combine male and female attributes and also their ability to maintain a close link with the spirit world. It is specifically in respect to the combination of male and female qualities that we see the importance of gender considerations in understanding bissu identity.

ENDNOTE

1. As this chapter is based on ethnographic data, I do not incorporate published material. A range of works that discuss bissu include the following: Andaya, 2000; Badaruddin, 1980; Blair & Blair, 1988; Graham, 2001b, 2003, 2004b, 2004c; Hamonic, 1975, 1977a, 1977b, 1980, 1987a, 1987b, 1988, 2002; Holt, 1939; Kennedy, 1993; Lathief, 2002; Lathief, Sutton, & Mohamad, 2001; Matthes, 1872; Sirk, 1975; Tomaszewski, Rush, & Graham, 2001; van der Kroef, 1956.

A Journey through Two Indonesian Weddings

I n Bugis, one term meaning to marry is *siala,* "to take each other." And, indeed, many Bugis view marriage as a reciprocal act where the bride and groom take each other to be lifelong partners. Marriage in South Sulawesi is not just a contractual agreement between two people, however, but it is a matter into which entire kin networks are drawn, renewing, strengthening, and establishing new alliances. As a reflection of the importance of marriage, weddings are the most celebrated events in Bugis society.

An elaborate wedding may take place over a number of weeks and witness the attendance of hundreds of guests. It is crucial then that all details of the wedding be in order. After all, it is through a successful wedding that a family can assert and affirm its social status. It is in ensuring the success of a wedding that the vital roles of bissu and calabai are fully realized. As such, an examination of Bugis weddings provides the perfect site for an ethnographic excursion into the social roles of bissu and calabai.

In order to carry out this exploration, this chapter is divided into two main sections. The first section describes a wedding that took place in Jakarta. As the bride was from a high-status Bugis family, it was deemed necessary to have bissu attend and perform a number of essential roles and ceremonies. Bissu were called upon to confirm the link between the nobility and their heavenly ancestors. Only bissu can do this because only bissu embody female and male elements, and this is necessary for them to communicate with the spirit world (see Chapter 6). This wedding, then, explores how bissu contribute to matrimonial ceremonies.

The second section describes a wedding that took place in the small town of Sengkang. Calabai played a central role in the organization and presentation of the wedding. As calabai are considered to combine desirable qualities of both women (e.g., creativity and patience) and men (e.g., strength and endurance), they are regarded as excellent wedding managers. As a reflection of this, calabai are often referred to by the respectful Bugis title *Indo' Botting* (Wedding Mother). This wedding reveals the crucial roles calabai assume in many Bugis weddings.

In this chapter, my goal is to present a detailed description of Bugis weddings that illuminates the important roles played by both bissu and calabai. Given its descriptive nature, it is no coincidence that the chapter is based on ethnographic material. This material is presented in the form of my own field notes and the narratives of various informants. Where appropriate, I incorporate published material, although there is a noticeable lack of this available, a fact that is somewhat surprising considering the significance of Bugis weddings. This paucity of research is, however, partly compensated for by the quality of the published sources.

The two most dedicated studies of Bugis weddings are Nurul Ilmi Idrus's excellent PhD dissertation, *"To Take Each Other": Bugis Practices of Gender, Sexuality and Marriage* (2003) and Susan Millar's outstanding ethnography, *Bugis Weddings* (1989). Smaller, though still highly valuable, contributions have been made by various other scholars. Christian Pelras's superb book, *The Bugis* (1996), outlines weddings. Sirtjo Koolhof (1999: 366) discusses a 1996 Bugis royal wedding in Jakarta. There are also historical documents detailing weddings. For instance, Nicolas Gervaise (1971: 105–116) describes marriage and divorce as he saw it in the seventeenth century. Other sources that touch on weddings in South Sulawesi include Chabot (1996) and Robinson and Paeni (1998). What is overlooked in all of this material, however, is a specific focus on the roles of bissu and calabai. I hope this chapter will begin to fill this void and develop an understanding of the roles of bissu and calabai in Bugis weddings.

A WEDDING IN JAKARTA: ROLES OF BISSU

Fortuitously, the great-niece of my host-grandmother married during my fieldwork period. While I attended many weddings, this wedding proved to be exceptional. Both the bride and groom were from extremely wealthy families, and their social status was very high. These two factors combined to ensure that the marriage of Andi Marawah and Bambang would be celebrated with an ostentatious display of wealth.

By hosting an elaborate wedding, the families of the bride and groom respectively reinforce their social location. As Millar (1989: 1) asserts, Bugis "weddings constitute fora in which competitive and hierarchical relations are momentarily articulated." Moreover, by performing the appropriate rites and displaying the garments, ornaments, and other accoutrements to which they are entitled, the bride and groom and their respective families assert their rank. As Pelras (1996: 159) notes, "[T]he identity, rank and number of guests bear witness to their [the respective families of the bride and groom] social connections and influence; and the wedding feast is an opportunity for both the bride's and bridegroom's families to display their wealth." Indeed, Andi Marawah and Bambang's wedding reportedly cost over US$60,000 and was attended by such Bugis notables as then Indonesian President B. J. Habibie, parliamentary figure Andi Mallarangeng, and business tycoon Andi Galib.

Andi Marawah had just turned 26, a birthday that she celebrated by graduating from the University of Indonesia with a master's degree. She is well traveled and spends some summers in England, where her aunt and uncle live. Along with her family, she has twice made the pilgrimage to Mecca. Until her marriage, Andi Marawah continued to live at home with her parents and three younger sisters in a lush, enclosed suburb in Jakarta. Andi Marawah occupied her own wing, where she had two maids and a chauffeur at her disposal. While she has never taken public transport or had any intimate experience of how most Indonesians live, she is not as pretentious as one might expect of someone who has grown up in this privileged environment.

Andi Marawah's father is the mayor (*walikota*) of a district in West Java. In addition to the advantages this brings in terms of wealth and opportunity, Andi Marawah's father is also a direct descendent of Bugis nobility. Indeed, the *Andi* before Marawah's name indicates her noble descent. While the particulars are confusing, Andi Marawah is the great-niece of Puang Sari. Until her death in July 2002, Puang Sari was regarded by Bugis as the Queen of Wajo', the district of which Sengkang, my main field site, is the capital. Indeed, Puang Sari's status was so high that she never married because there was no man of high enough status for her to marry. Andi Marawah's father is also the first cousin of ex-President Habibie—although the specifics of this are unclear, some people say that Habibie was adopted into this family. Running through Andi Marawah's veins, then, is pure white blood, the symbolic marker of Bugis nobility. An unsuitable marriage would result in Andi Marawah's children having diluted white blood. This would lower her family's social standing and cause her family to feel great shame (*siri'*, B). Only a suitable groom, therefore, could entertain hopes of marrying Andi Marawah.

Since her birth, Andi Marawah's family have discussed desirable marriage alliances and evaluated prospective grooms. Andi Marawah's marriage would not be left to chance. Here the relationship between a purely arranged marriage and a marriage based on affection becomes blurred. Andi Marawah realized that she could never marry the son of a pedicab (*becak*) driver, for instance, without suffering severe repercussions, which may have included her being disowned by her family. But Andi Marawah had no desire to marry someone of lower socioeconomic status anyway. In this sense, her expectations aligned with those of her family. From within a select pool of prospective suitors, then, Andi Marawah was free to choose her own partner.

Just as a side note, arranged marriages do still occur in Bugis society, although the definition of "arranged" is somewhat more flexible now than in the past, and prospective brides and grooms usually have some say in their marriages. While in Jakarta, I became friends with another of Puang Sari's great-nieces, Bau Ning. Along with her mother and aunts, we spent quite a bit of time jokingly appraising possible matches for Bau Ning. Bau Ning was in a complex situation. Her social status is high, higher even than Andi Marawah's, and as such, prospective grooms had to undergo rigorous genealogical examination to ensure that their pure white blood had never been tainted with commoner red blood. In these informal discussions, however, socioeconomic status and job prospects were assessed far more frequently than bloodline or ethnicity. I recently received an invitation to Bau Ning's wedding. While she barely knew the groom, it was an arranged marriage that she accepted; if Bau Ning had declined the match, the marriage would not have been enforced.

When Bambang got married, he was 32 years old and had a prestigious and well-paying job in the private sector. Being the eldest son of a high-ranking army general granted Bambang many opportunities in life, such as the chance to secure a good education. While Bambang and his immediate family identify as Javanese, Bambang's great-grandfather was a Bugis man from South Sulawesi. As such, Bambang's impending marriage held a sense of welcoming a "regional child" (*anak daerah*) back into the Bugis fold. When Bambang was introduced to Andi Marawah over two years ago, it was love at first sight, according to how Bambang now tells the tale. Since then the couple have been slowly developing a solid foundation on which to base their marriage.

While the elaborate festivities that were sure to accompany this wedding made it an attractive event to witness, there was a more compelling reason for my enthusiastic acceptance of Puang Sari's invitation to accompany her to Jakarta. Because of the noble status of the bride's family, the attendance of two bissu, Mariani and Haji Baco', was requested to sanctify the marriage and provide information on how an authentic Bugis wedding ought to be performed—many people thought that living in Jakarta, Andi Marawah's family would have forgotten all about proper Bugis traditions.

Another reason why bissu were required to attend this wedding relates to Bugis mythology. In the La Galigo epic cycle, bissu facilitated the first earthly marriage between Wé Nyili' Timo and Batara Guru. The power of bissu to bring about this union cements for many people the idea that bissu are the embodiments of auspicious powers, an attribute especially useful in blessing weddings. Bissu are believed to have originally descended to earth with the first white-blooded rulers, who were descendents of the gods. The connection between these noble rulers and bissu remains strong. Indeed, bissu continue to mediate between the nobility and the gods, and it is precisely this function, and the performance of particular associated rites, that helps ensure the perpetuation of the sacred white blood. There is no time where the perpetuation of white blood must be guaranteed more than at a wedding, and consequently bissu are required to ensure this. As

Andaya (2000: 44) notes, in this way, "bissu confirm their intermediary role between the human community and the world of the gods, and reaffirm their crucial function in assuring the survival of those of white blood."

First word of the impending marriage came in early September:

1st September, 1999. This morning I went to visit Haji Baco' expecting to be ensnared for hours by mythological stories that s/he insists on relating in a bewildering mix of Indonesian, Bugis, and the sacred bissu language. Haji Baco' must be well over 60 years old and is not the most endearing person I've ever met. Whenever I go there, s/he always just says, "Enter (Masuk). Sit (Duduk)." Then we sit in silence until hir niece brings us tea. After the first sip, Haji Baco' tells me what s/he is going to teach me today, and then s/he launches into an extensive narrative. I always tape these sessions, as Haji Baco' insists I do, but when I take them back to Puang Sari's, no one there can understand much better than I can what Haji Baco' is talking about because of the jumbled languages s/he uses. At some point in the narrative, Haji Baco' always abruptly stops and tells me that is enough for today. S/he then gives me a date and time when I should return. I frequently go a whole session barely saying a word. Haji Baco' knows a great deal about the Bugis past, and s/he is respected as a source of information. In fact, Haji Baco' was the royal bissu until the courts were disbanded by the Indonesian government not so long ago. S/he continues to have influence, as well. When I arrived there this morning, however, hir niece told me that I had just missed hir; s/he was on hir way to Puang Sari's! I raced back to the road and hailed another becak. *On arrival I made my way up the hill to find Haji Baco' waiting for an audience with Puang Sari. Finally, Haji Baco' was ushered in to Puang Sari's room, and I was allowed to follow and listen to the conversation. There is to be a wedding. Puang Sari's great-niece, Andi Marawah, is marrying the son of an army general. The bridewealth consists of* sompa *(B, a symbolic sum of money) and* dui' mēnrē *(B, spending money), and these are amounts of money given to the bride by the groom's family. It is said that the bridewealth is Rp300 million (US$30,000)! Andi Marawah's father is the mayor of a district in West Java and he's referred to as Pak Walikota. Pak Walikota apparently wants the wedding of his eldest child to be an authentic (asli) Bugis wedding. He has requested that Puang Sari arrange for two bissu to go to Jakarta to perform a number of important functions and ensure that traditional practices are followed. Haji Baco' has officiated at all of Puang Sari's relatives' weddings, and s/he is referred to as the court bissu. In addition to Haji Baco', Mariani, the highest-ranking bissu in South Sulawesi, has also been requested to attend the wedding. Puang Sari told Haji Baco' to call on Mariani and relate this information. Haji Baco' is to return to Puang Sari's in one week.*

So began a month of wedding preparations. As instructed, one week after their initial meeting, Haji Baco' returned to Puang Sari's house:

7th September. Haji Baco' has returned with Mariani to see Puang Sari. Earlier this evening Haji Baco', Mariani, two of Mariani's companions (pendamping), and I sat on the floor below Puang Sari's bed. Most of the discussion centered on what materials bissu need to bring to Jakarta. Bissu will be responsible for bringing the sacred cloth (lamming, B) that will decorate the bridal table and the bedroom. They must also bring all of their regalia, such as Mariani's sacred sheath (tapi', B) and sword (alamang, B), musical instruments, and various other paraphernalia. Mariani and Haji Baco' have been asked to come back in five days' time to arrange departure dates.

14th September. Departure date has been set at some time around the start of October. It has also been decided that I will travel with Haji Baco' down to Pangkep, pick up Mariani, and help them with all of the paraphernalia that need to go to Jakarta. The three of us will then go to Makassar and stay the night at a relative's house. Then the following morning, possibly 5th October, we will rendezvous with everyone at the harbor, and Suki, one of the young women traveling with us, will pass out boat tickets.

18th September. I went to Haji Baco''s this morning. S/he is organizing things to take to Jakarta. So far there are two sacks full of decorative materials. These will go around the walls of the wedding room and the bridal chamber. There are also a lot of cake covers (bosora', B) and silk sarongs (cenramata sabbé, B).

4th October. Departure day has arrived. I went to Haji Baco's house at 6 a.m. this morning because we were supposed to catch a bus at 6:30 a.m., but the bus was late by two hours! Not only was the bus late but it was full, and we had to jam three sacks into it, as well as ourselves. It was only 100 km to Pangkep, yet it took us a staggering five hours because of frequent pick-ups and drop-offs and detours; it certainly wasn't due to a lack of speed because the driver was a maniac who was constantly trying to make up for lost time. We alighted at Pangkep to find Mariani waiting very anxiously. We hailed another bus and crammed in again. The place where we are staying is on the outskirts of Makassar, so when we disembarked we had to hire a mini bus because all our belongings would not fit into a taxi, even though we were now 10 kilograms lighter because two bags were mistakenly left on the bus. Tomorrow morning we are off to Jakarta.

6th October. We met up with everyone at the harbor yesterday morning—except Puang Sari who flew to Jakarta. Suki handed out our tickets, and I read with horror that they said, "Without Sleeping Berth" ("Tanpa Tempat Tidur"). In effect, this meant that we had to find a place in the corridor where we could spread out for the three days and two nights it will take to reach Jakarta. The ship can accommodate 2000 passengers, but the rumor running around the corridors is that it is overloaded, and there are 5000 passengers on board. This does not particularly surprise me, as there is literally no floor space left in the entire ship; even the stairwells and stairs are covered with bodies. I was even more horrified when I realized that to check tickets (something they do after each docking), the crew locks all the access doors. So for two hours a day, there is a period when our section of the ship, which is below the water line, is locked, and if there is an emergency of any kind, we will have no escape route. I am trying to console myself, however, with the fact that I have a captive audience in Mariani and Haji Baco', and this is a perfect opportunity to seek some good information.

7th October. We docked in the port of Jakarta safe and sound around noon today after far too many days at sea. What a contrast our reception at the harbor *was to our position on the ship. Pak Walikota had arranged for a number of escorts and four coaches to greet us and take us to a leafy, secure complex in a wealthy Jakarta suburb. After so long in Sengkang, the palatial homes of this area have left me stunned. For the guests who had never left Sulawesi, this show of staggering wealth must be quite astounding. The people who live in this complex are all important and wealthy officials and dignitaries; a number of them have offered up their homes to accommodate this sudden influx of Bugis relatives. I, along with fourteen others, occupy the south wing of Pak Walikota's house.*

The day after arriving in Jakarta, everyone was issued with instructions on what needed to be prepared for the wedding. While the higher-status guests from Sulawesi were exempt from this work and spent the next few days shopping and sightseeing—indeed Pak Walikota hired coaches to take guests on tours, including to Taman Mini and Safari Park—for others, especially bissu, the work of organizing a wedding did not allow this luxury. Such a demarcation is a striking example of the importance of rank.

8th October. I received the Committee Composition and Wedding Agenda (Susunan Panitia dan Acara Pernikahan) today. It is a thirty-page book! I can barely imagine how much work will go into this wedding to ensure its success. Mariani and Haji Baco' started preparing special kinds of candles today to decorate the pavilion (baruga). Indeed, carpenters are busy right now in the front yard building the pavilion that will be used for the cleansing ceremony. The agenda states such things as, "By 0930, 9th October, the following have to be arranged: all the officials, including the transport, decoration, ceremony, documentation, and parking officials, have to be present; the adat *instruments have to be arranged; the decorations erected; and all of the offerings, including jackfruit, candles, chili paste, and sarongs, need to be gathered." The wedding festivities and ceremonies will last two weeks.*

9th October. I am getting the feeling that bissu are being ignored. I guess everyone is so busy with what they have to do that everyone is just left to their own tasks. But bissu almost seem like an anachronism. Adat *is certainly very important or bissu would not have been brought all the way here from Sulawesi; I think they are getting paid around Rp1.5 million (US$150). But I get the sense that bissu rituals are seen as something that must be performed rather than something that people actually want to bother with.*

10th October. It is 8 p.m. and quite a few women and men (about fifty) are sitting on the floor discussing the arrival of the groom on the wedding day. Each person has a name plaque in front of him or her, and there are two microphones being passed around. One of the central issues being discussed is how to get the elaborate rituals completed quickly enough so that President Habibie is not detained for too long. Another issue being discussed is where to seat the President. The term protokol istana *(palace protocol) is continually referred to, and on these points Haji Baco' and Mariani's opinion is sought. After the bissu detailed traditional seating arrangements, Pak Mohamed, one of the high-ranking guests who is also helping organize the wedding, proposed an alternative:*

PAK MOHAMED: Now, traditionally, as the bissu have just told us, we have one long table of sweets, and people sit on the floor alongside it. But I would like to suggest a change. What about if we organize the tables like this? [He starts reshuffling the tables]. Now, the most important thing is that the guests feel that they are special and that they go away feeling spoiled (*manja*). How about if instead of having a long impersonal table, we arrange them so that people sit in smaller groups around smaller tables with only four people?

IBU FATMA: Oh, no, we couldn't do that. It's not tradition, and because it's not tradition, it's not appropriate (*tidak cocok*).

IBU WULAN: Yeah, that's right! And how could we even fit forty officials in with a seating arrangement like that? President Habibie, Andi Galib, and Andi Mallarangeng all have to fit in, you know.

While Pak Mohamed's new seating arrangement was eventually decided upon, it is noteworthy that bissu were asked to provide information on how seating arrangements were traditionally organized. Indeed, from this point on bissu began to play a more central role in the wedding. This was partly because bissu demonstrated their knowledge of tradition during the discussion on seating arrangements and partly because people who had not previously been acquainted with bissu now saw how they formed a vital part of wedding organization.

> *11th October. It is the start of the official ceremonies and rituals. Tonight was the* mappatudang (B), *which was a ceremony where Puang Sari, as the highest-ranking relative, was asked to give permission for the wedding to take place. The parents of the bride approached Puang Sari and sought her permission for the marriage to go ahead. Mariani then went over to Puang Sari and, with hir sword, sought a blessing for the marriage from Puang Sari and transferred this blessing to Andi Marawah. This happened by trapping Puang Sari's good blessing in the sword and then taking the sword to Andi Marawah, where the good blessing was released and it entered Andi Marawah.*
>
> *12th October. Up again at 5 a.m. No reason, just for the fun of waking up, apparently. Every morning we sing karaoke, of all things—so I couldn't stay asleep even if I wanted to—and eat doughnuts and drink sweet tea. There are a number of ceremonies today, including assembling the pavilion* (pemasangan baruga, B); *a prayer reading in the center of the house; setting a chicken free in the yard to ward off catastrophe* (tolak bala); *and well-wishing. At 7:30 a.m. we started preparing the first offering* (sesaji). *This offering consists of special types of cake* (béppa ugi', B), *like onde-onde* (B); *different types of rice, like* sokko' palopo' (B), ka'do' minynya' (B), *and* nanré puté (B); *chicken; and a few other things, like an incense-offering mixture* (adduppa-duppang, B). *There were many types of fruit, all specifically named, like king bananas* (pisang raja). *Bissu were primarily responsible for gathering and arranging the offerings, and they composed a list and ordered people to collect the required ingredients. Mariani set up the bath place* (ma'barumbung, B) *today. S/he also made* masé pelleng

(B), *which are long candlestick things made from candlenut* (kemiri). *Mariani sat surrounded by eggs, cinnamon, red sugar,* sirih *leaves, coconuts, and puffed rice. At one point a man came over to ask Mariani something and referred to hir as* Mas (title for a man, like "Sir"). *Mariani looked quite offended at being addressed by a man's label, and someone sitting nearby yelled out, "Don't call hir* Mas!" *Haji Baco' was close by, filling a large clay pot with coal and incense, which will later be set under the bath place to create a sauna effect. All the while that this was happening, two women sat in the background melodiously chanting Islamic prayers; it was seductively beautiful. Before, not many people were clear on the roles of bissu because they were raised in Java. Now that the role of bissu is becoming so central, bissu are receiving much more respect; for instance, people are coming and asking them questions about how things ought to be done.*

13th October. Today's ceremonies included mappaisseng (B) *and* mappēsau (B). Mappaisseng *involves the passing of information (literally "to cause to know"), while* mappēsau *refers to a special herbal steam bath. For the steam bath, Andi Marawah sat in a plastic enclosure and under her stool was the coal pot Haji Baco' had previously made. The steam surrounded Andi Marawah and gave her skin a lovely smell* (mengharumkan pengantin). *Traditionally, the bride would be enclosed in a bark dome, and she would be seated upstairs in her room. Under the house, a bamboo pipe would connect the dome to a fire and the smoke would rise up the pipe, infusing the bride's skin with a beautiful scent* (mabbarumbung, B). *During the bath, bissu sat chanting on either side of Andi Marawah.*

14th October. This morning the bride had water splashed over her in a ceremony called **mappacemmé** *(B, literally "to bathe someone"). The washing place* (tempat siram) *cost Rp1.7 million (US$170) to construct—a lot considering a civil servant earns around Rp500,000 a month. The ceremony started with bissu going to Andi Marawah's room and leading her outside to the washing place. After Andi Marawah was seated, Mariani and Haji Baco' sat on either side of her. Andi Marawah's parents and ten family members then used a ladle to pour, and a branch to splash, sacred water over her. The sacred water was from seven regions in Sulawesi brought in vases by seven different people. While the water was being splashed, Islamic prayers were recited, and a short speech was said. After this, respected family members fed Andi Marawah a mixture of coconut and red sugar—later we all fought over what was left because if you eat this, you will marry quickly. Bissu then led Andi Marawah back to her room where she changed out of her outfit, which was partly made from small flowers* (kembang sedap malam), *into a white Islamic gown. After the* mappacemmé *ceremony, the bride cannot be touched by any man except her father because she is now considered cleansed* (**suci**)—*this does not apply to bissu, who can still touch the bride because bissu are considered to be very* suci. *Meanwhile, all the guests moved inside to the reception hall and took a seat on the floor around the cake stands and we had morning tea.*

The next ceremony for the day was a prayer reading called Khatam al-Qur'an dan Pengajian. *Two women started clashing cymbals, and all the assembled women began to read from the prayer books that had been handed out.*

Andi Marawah, who was sitting on a raised platform with her three sisters and two Qur'an specialists, then began reading from the Qur'an. A Muslim bride should show she is capable of reading the Qur'an before being allowed to marry. Bissu sat on the floor in front of the platform on which Andi Marawah was sitting.

The first of the evening's ceremonies was mappacci (B). *Andi Marawah dressed in yet another costume, the third for the day, and then sat on her bed along with her immediate family. Haji Baco' and Mariani knelt in front of her, and using a microphone that broadcast into the street, proceeded to seek permission from the spirits (dewata) to bless Andi Marawah's impending marriage. Both bissu then chanted in the sacred bissu language for a few minutes. Having thus contacted dewata, Mariani extended a rope (***lawolo,*** B) to Andi Marawah and, following Haji Baco', led Andi Marawah out to the pavilion. Andi Marawah climbed into the pavilion while four girls held a silk umbrella over her. Andi Marawah laid her hands on the* dara muse (B), *which was an arrangement consisting of nine sarongs (cenramata, B) and young coconut leaves (janur), both symbols of fertility. Bissu stood in front of the pavilion and held the* lawolo *across it and recited a number of incantations, requesting the spirits to bestow fertility on Andi Marawah. Mariani and Haji Baco' then stood on either side of the pavilion (Figure 7.1). In turn, respected family members were called to approach Andi Marawah and offer her their own blessing. Haji Hasanuddin and his wife were called over the microphone first, and two girls dressed in wedding costumes came and led them to the pavilion. The couple then knelt in front of Andi Marawah and, dipping their fingers in a henna mix (pacci, B), rubbed it into Andi Marawah's palms. The last people called were Andi Marawah's immediate family, and it all became a very moving time, with everyone getting teary eyed. Bissu then started chanting again, and Andi Marawah's parents and sisters moved in to sit under the umbrella with her. Bissu contacted the spirits again to finalize the blessing and bring this ceremony to a close. Bissu then rose and led Andi Marawah and her family back to Andi Marawah's room.*

It was then time for the mappanré ade' (B) *ceremony. Andi Marawah sat on the foot of her bed, while her parents and sisters sat at the head. Mariani and Haji Baco' flanked Andi Marawah. This ceremony also requested a blessing from Allah before the official marriage takes place tomorrow. Bissu chanted softly, and Andi Marawah's father told her how proud he is of her and how much he loves her. Andi Marawah then tried to respond, fighting back tears: "Thank you for respecting my choice of husband, and I hope that I can always make you proud. I love (sayang) you all." Bissu performed one more chant, which signaled the finish of today's ceremonies. At the end of this, many people came up to the bissu and shook their hands in recognition of the important role they had performed.*

In all of these ceremonies, bissu assumed key roles. In the first ritual recounted, Mariani was required to receive a blessing from Puang Sari and confer this blessing, which was stored within Mariani's sword, on Andi Marawah. This practice reveals the importance of status in Bugis weddings. Puang Sari was sought to bless the wedding because she was the highest-ranking person

FIGURE 7.1 Bissu flanking a bride at a pre-marriage fertility blessing

in attendance, but it was only bissu who could transfer the blessing from Puang Sari to Andi Marawah. Puang Sari could not directly convey the blessing because she did not have a connection with the spirit world, and thus her blessing would have been ineffective. For the next ritual, it was bissu who prepared all of the offerings. Moreover, bissu were the only individuals who knew what ingredients were required for each offering. Such was the authority of bissu that they were able to order people to seek out specific ingredients. During the herbal steam bath, bissu led the bride out of her bedroom and flanked her during the ritual. Similarly, bissu sat below the bride during the prayer reading. In the next event, bissu sought permission from *dewata* for the *mappacci* fertility blessing to take place; this blessing should precede any official Bugis marriage ceremony. Bissu are the only individuals able to mediate with the spirit world and thus seek the blessing of *dewata*. It is the combination of male and female elements that enables bissu to contact *dewata* (this was discussed more fully in Chapter 6). The final ritual involved bissu performing a chant, the end of which signaled that the official marriage ceremony could take place.

> *15th October. The official wedding (akad nikah) day has arrived. It is 9 a.m., and Mariani and Haji Baco' are trying to secure microphones to their tops. The ceremony will be broadcast for the whole street to hear. Military guards are everywhere, and the complex has been cordoned off because not only are the bride and groom from important families but there are many notable dignitaries attending. Hundreds of guests have already arrived—a large pavilion has been*

FIGURE 7.2 Bissu leading a groom to his bride

*erected in the street to seat most of the guests, as only the most important will be
seated inside. This appropriation of public space is commonly seen during
weddings in Indonesia. The groom has just arrived, along with his substantial
entourage, and he is being led toward the house by both bissu (Figure 7.2). Andi
Marawah is in seclusion (dipingit) inside the house. Before the groom can enter
the house, he must first overcome a number of challenges. Mariani and Haji Baco'
have spent a long time setting up the obstacle course that the groom must complete
before he can enter the house. While we were waiting for the groom to arrive,
Mariani explained to me what the obstacle course involves:*

Well, it's like this, you see. The groom and his entourage (*pendamping*)
all come in a line, and all the people in front of the groom carry wedding
presents. When the groom gets here in his car, I will go over and invite
him out of the car, and if he wants to get out, he will take hold of the
other end of a thick, braided rope called *lawolo*. Then we walk to the
obstacle course and I lead him through it, but I try and make him fail.
Like, I will try to make it hard, make him not want to go on with the
course. There are many obstacles. The first one involves fire, and the
groom has to walk over fire (*bila ri mangke'*, B). Then he has to walk
down a white sheet, and then he comes to the next obstacle. The white
sheet keeps his feet clean and pure. After the sheet is walked on, it's called
ridanguwaté (B). The groom then has to walk under a bamboo arch
(*menrawé*, B), and it's made of ten pairs of bamboo poles that make a long

A-frame structure. Chickens have to walk through this too. The next obstacle is a bamboo tree that is decorated with ribbons (*aratiga,* B). The groom has to break it down. If the groom breaks it down, then he won't have any troubles and he will be successful. Next, the groom has to stand under an umbrella and I chant to him; Haji Baco' chants too. Then there's a buffalo head, which symbolizes wealth and prosperity, that has just been severed; it's on a platform called *denrakatu* (B). Next is a mud pie in a bowl called *tana menroja* (B), and the groom has to step on it to leave his footprint. The dirt is from the parents' of the groom and bride birthplaces. It's mixed with coconut milk. The reason it is all mixed up is to make a good, strong connection and relationship between the parents and the bride and groom. Then there's a clay pot (*umpa sikate,* B), and the groom has to smash it and this shows strength, but he has to be careful because there's an egg in the pot and he can't break the egg; he has to show controlled strength. Then there's a sarong (*lipa patola,* B, literally "a sarong made of cloth from India"), and the groom has to touch it to ensure fertility and we bissu splash water on him. Then after the groom makes it through the obstacle course, a hundred boys and girls come with gifts. And then he can enter the house. Oh, but there's one more thing . . . the talking between *dewata* and the groom and bissu (*ma'lawolo,* B).

Mariani notes that the last challenge involves talking with *dewata* (**ma'lawolo**). *Ma'lawolo* is a part of the wedding ritual where the bissu interrogates the groom concerning his status (cf. Robinson, 1998: 288). In the following exchange, Mariani is possessed by *dewata,* and s/he is speaking with Haji Baco'. They are seeking permission for the marriage to take place:

DEWATA: Who are you to be calling me?

 BISSU: It is me. I am requesting permission to bring this man into the
        house of his bride and for the two to marry. We want to come to
        your house. Let this groom meet his bride so that they can be married.

DEWATA: Where are you from?

 BISSU: We are from Luwu' and from Boné. We are your children.

Possessed by *dewata,* Mariani then chants the marriage proposal on behalf of the groom's side:

Assalam Alaikum Warahmatullahi Wabarakatuh
Ooooh Rue Lawoloē Lawalenrēng
My Lord,
God of Fire who lives in the heavens
We believe in Your truth and in Your decision
And we seek Your blessing
From above the water drops
From below the smoke rises
If broken into pieces it is left in ruin

Clever it is to follow the course of the river
Even in the river's bends bushes grow
We want to ask you
Would you let us stay in your house
While the sun and moon are visible
Soon the noble light will appear
Amen

This chant was spoken by Mariani in the sacred bissu language, and s/he later translated it into Indonesian for me to understand.

During this dialogue, Mariani held one end of the *lawolo* while the groom held the other. According to Pelras (1996: 158), the braiding of the *lawolo* symbolizes the "rainbow of *La Galigo* times, as well as the mythic *Welenréng* tree which linked the Earth, here represented by the groom's party, to heaven, represented by the bride's house." In this conceptualization, the bride is considered to be closer to heaven than is the groom. This understanding ties into notions of women being defined by concerns of *siri'* and white blood, while men must undergo challenging obstacles in order to prove their masculinity and their worthiness to marry a high-status bride. Indeed, Greg Acciaioli (personal communication, 2002) has noted that there seems to be almost a contradiction in the roles of bissu. On the one hand, bissu facilitate the wedding and ensure that both partners desire each other and that the deities approve of the marriage. On the other hand, bissu construct an obstacle course that the groom must overcome in order to marry the bride. My interpretation of this is that bissu must be persuaded of the worth of the groom. If he shows strength, endurance, and intelligence, he has proven himself to be worthy of the bride. With confidence in the groom, bissu are then convinced that the marriage is worth blessing. Ilmi Idrus (personal communication, 2006) has also told me that the obstacles are put in place to guarantee that it is extremely difficult for a man to marry a woman (*susahnya mengawini seorang perempuan*). The obstacles also ensure that later in their marriage, when conflict arises, the couple just needs to remember all the obstacles they initially had to get through to get married, and their current conflict will seem relatively minor.

In reply to Mariani's marriage proposal on behalf of the groom, Haji Baco' responded for the bride's side:

Ooooh Rue Lawoloē Lawalenrēng
My Lord,
The fire of God lives in the heavens
Oh your soul is of noble descent
With honor you may climb the ladder
Go to my room, may the Raja not curse you
The blessed are received in the palace
Like a fish hook anchoring deep into the sea
Love is like an anchor
Be happy and I welcome you with great happiness
In order that the noble light will clearly appear

Thus convinced that the groom is welcome, bissu lead him into the house. Pelras (1996: 158) similarly found, "Once convinced that the bridegroom was indeed a descendent of Tompo' Tikka, Wéwang Nriwu' and Luwu', representing the east, west, and center of the world respectively, the bissu gently pulling on the *lawolo,* drew the bridegroom upstairs under a show of scattered puffed rice."

By possessing bissu, *dewata* are able to attend the wedding, as Haji Yamin explains:

> Before and now, wedding ceremonies were and are performed by bissu. The *dewata* is invited to the wedding of the Raja, but the spirit has no human form. Bissu must call and invite the *dewata* to enter the bissu's body. So the *dewata* attends the wedding living in the body of the bissu. If the bissu were a man or a woman, the *dewata* couldn't enter because we don't know if the *dewata* is a man or a woman. So *dewata* can enter bissu because bissu are both man and woman.

Soon we were all inside the main house with the groom, the groom's retainers, President Habibie, and Pak Walikota sitting at the main table.

> *The groom and his future father-in-law locked thumbs and the latter asked, "Will you take my daughter as your wife and respect and cherish her for your entire life?" The groom responded with such incredible speed that the reply came out as, "YesItakeyourdaughterandwillprotectherwithallmylifeAmen." Indeed, the groom must respond in a single breath or the marriage is not valid. Everyone laughed and cheered and yelled out, "Alhamdulillah." I could hear laughter coming from all the way up the street. Even the President laughed. Next, the groom was given a gold ring and a book* (buku hikmah). *The President acted as the witness and signed the documentation. At that point, they were officially married. The groom rose and went to Andi Marawah's door. When she opened it, she asked for money and received it. Bissu then led the groom into the bridal chamber. Bissu joined the couple's hands* (mappasikarawa, B), *but only after Andi Marawah had tried valiantly to resist the groom's hand. Bissu then began a chant and wrapped the couple in a sarong and sewed them up* (jarungpulaweng, B). *The couple then had to jump up and Andi Marawah was the first up, which made everybody laugh because this means that she will be the leader in the marriage. Next, the couple gave each other rings* (tukar cincin). *Bissu then led them out of the room and toward the bride's parents. The group exchanged salutations, and bissu knelt in front of the couple and blessed them with a sacred sword, thus sealing the marriage. All the guests then filed past the newlyweds, congratulating them and offering cash donations* (massolo', B). *Later that night, attention continued to be given to the newlyweds, and many of the guests sat out in the front of the house and reported with glee how many times the en suite light in the bridal chamber came on—three times. This is supposed to indicate the number of times the marriage was consummated because of the prescription of washing after intercourse.*

In these ceremonies we again see the central role of bissu. Bissu had to become possessed by *dewata* in order to interrogate the groom and ensure he was worthy of marrying the bride. Having proved this, bissu then led the groom to the official wedding ceremony.

The final ceremony accompanying Andi Marawah and Bambang's wedding was the reception:

> *17th October. Tonight was the reception* (resepsi). *A huge conference center was rented and elaborately decorated. Pak Walikota hired the forty most beautiful female and male youths* (pemuda) *in Indonesia. They wore traditional Bugis dress* (baju bodo, B), *and their task was to receive the hundreds of guests who came to pay their respects to the newlyweds. At the appropriate hour, bissu entered the hall and started performing a chant and a ritual dance. The bride and groom then followed, walking under an umbrella supported by four girls. The couple were wearing Bugis wedding clothes, but they were white. Bissu then led the couple through the vanguard of guests, dancing as they went in order to ward off evil spirits. When they reached the stage, the bride and groom, along with their entourage, waited in the wings while bissu performed a cleansing ceremony. This involved bissu performing the self-stabbing ritual* (ma'giri', B) *as proof that they were possessed by powerful spirits and could thus bless the wedding. The wedding party then came on stage and sat in a horseshoe shape. Bissu took their place seated at the couple's feet, a position they held throughout the evening* (Figure 7.3). *In turn, all of the guests came on stage and offered their congratulations to Andi Marawah and Bambang and their respective families.*

Thus, the wedding came to a close. Andi Marawah and Bambang headed off to Venice for their honeymoon, and Mariani, Haji Baco', and myself, along with the other 300 members of our group, returned to Sulawesi aboard the infamous Pelni ship. Bissu had performed their role successfully; their inclusion in the wedding signifying the continuing importance of bissu and traditional Bugis customs.

A WEDDING IN SENGKANG: ROLES OF CALABAI

> You can't have a wedding without calabai. Impossible! Calabai are the organizers (*pengurus*) and managers (*pengatur*) of weddings; we cook, we decorate, we dress the bride and groom. Oh, and don't forget, we're the entertainment...Wardut!
>
> YANTI, A CALABAI IN HIR 40s

True to Yanti's assertion, I rarely attended a wedding in South Sulawesi that was not organized to some extent by calabai. Indeed, at many weddings *wardut* was a real highlight. *Wardut* is an acronym of **wanita pria dangdut** (women man dangdut). *Waria* is an Indonesian variant of calabai, and *dangdut* is the name given to a genre of popular music heavily influenced by Hindi/Arabic melodies. So *wardut* is calabai performing a type of popular music.

F I G U R E 7.3 Bissu sitting before a newly married couple

Weddings form an arena in which calabai can claim a legitimate place in Bugis society. In recognition of the vital work they perform, calabai are often referred to as *Indo' Botting* (B, Wedding Mother)—although women are also referred to as *Indo' Botting*. One of the best ways to appreciate calabai identity is through an examination of Bugis weddings. As such, this section follows the wedding of Batari and Cakara, two individuals from lower-class Sengkang families. Their wedding provides a way to explore the roles calabai undertake at Bugis weddings.

Before delving into the details of this wedding, it is worth commenting on the discrepancy between my fieldwork findings and those of Susan Millar, who has conducted a comprehensive study of Bugis weddings. The starkest difference between our work relates to our respective positioning of calabai. In Millar's ethnography, calabai are virtually absent. Rather than playing a central role, as they do in my experience of Bugis weddings, in Millar's analysis calabai are mentioned only in passing. Moreover, Millar refers to calabai as ***kawé-kawé***, a term that my informants told me is a Makassar word describing a subjectivity similar, though not identical, to calabai: "The male costume specialists are frequently transvestites [*kawé-kawé* (B)] who present themselves as bisexual or androgynous individuals" (Millar, 1989: 83).

There are a number of possible reasons for our different positioning of calabai. First, Millar specifically focused on social status and used weddings as a way of demonstrating the importance of this aspect of Bugis life. As a result, Millar may have tended to overlook the roles of calabai (and bissu) in weddings. In a similar way, my own focus on gender may explain why I have recorded calabai (and bissu) playing such prominent roles. Indeed, as I tended to get invited to weddings where calabai (and bissu) were working, there is an obvious bias in my work.

I did, however, attend around sixty weddings in Sulawesi and one in Jakarta. Approximately forty-five of these had either calabai (or bissu) employed in some capacity. Any bias in my work is, therefore, reduced in light of the high number of weddings I attended.

Second, at the time of my fieldwork, Sulawesi was undergoing a revival of *adat* (traditional customs). As calabai and bissu are both considered experts in traditional knowledge and customs, this revival is likely to have contributed to the increased participation of calabai (and bissu) at weddings. While during my fieldwork calabai were involved in weddings, in Millar's field site of Soppeng, it is possible that during the early eighties, when Millar was conducting her field research, calabai did not play a major role in weddings there. This would account for Millar's cursory mention of calabai. Calabai, though, have been involved in weddings in Sengkang for as far back as people can remember; a number of calabai have worked as *Indo' Botting* since the 1940s.

Planning a Bugis wedding is a long and involved process. It requires many drawn-out negotiations and a great deal of complex planning. Although Batari and Cakara grew up in the same town and have known of each other since they were little, the formal proscription against intimate contact between unmarried couples meant that Batari and Cakara never had the opportunity to get to know each other well. It was, therefore, their respective families who first suggested the possibility of their marriage. Negotiations were thus undertaken by familial delegations, which did not directly include either the future bride or groom or their parents. While their wedding was arranged, it was an arrangement to which both Batari and Cakara agreed.

During the initial stage of proposing marriage, direct questions by either Batari or Cakara's family were avoided so as to save face if either party did not wish for the marriage to go ahead. When it became clear that both families in principle supported the marriage, the first formal step was taken. This involved the groom's delegation going to Batari's house to initiate negotiations. This initiation is referred to as *madduta* (B). At this meeting, the genealogy, rank, kinship, and assets of each party were examined. Moreover, as in any Bugis wedding, bridewealth was negotiated. As noted earlier, bridewealth is made up of two parts: *sompa* (B), which is a symbolic sum of money; and *dui' menre'* (B, spending money), which pays for the groom's contribution to the wedding. In addition, *lise' kawing* (B, wedding contents) and *mahar* (bridal gift) were negotiated. After these aspects were discussed, a date was fixed for the ratification of these amounts. At that ceremony, the wedding date was confirmed, and the gifts were passed around for examination. Batari and Cakara were never present at any of these discussions; rather, they were represented by delegations from their family.

After all of these negotiations had been formalized, preparations for the marriage ceremonies (*mappa'botting*, B, "to make the wedding") commenced. There were many ceremonies, and they took place over a week. The preparations for these ceremonies were exhaustive. In the following narrative, Batari's aunt, Ibu Tungke', talks about the early stages of organizing her niece's wedding:

This wedding has been planned for quite a while, you know. Sometimes weddings happen quickly, like Nurhayati's, which was quick, two weeks! But this one has been well planned. The bride is the first daughter and the groom is the first son, so, you know, it's an important wedding. Once it was decided that there would be a wedding, and that took a long time, you know we had to have all those meetings (*mappettuada*, B) where we couldn't really say it, you know, that the two should get married. Also there was all that talk about exchange of bridewealth and this involved accepting the marriage proposal and there were all those formal meetings between the groom's and the bride's families. Well, anyway, when that was all decided, we straight away went to Yulia [a calabai] because s/he has to agree with the date, right, to make sure it's a good date; everyone has to agree. This should be done straight away because calabai can be booked up for months. As soon as it's agreed that there will be a wedding, you must go at once to a calabai.

While Ibu Tungke' describes many of the important processes involved in the organization of Batari and Cakara's wedding, the one of most interest to this book is the role assumed by calabai. As Ibu Tungke' notes, contacting a calabai was the first priority after the wedding had been officially agreed to. It is important to ensure calabai are available to assist in wedding preparations because their particular constitution is believed to make them ideally suited to this type of work, as Sukmawati, a civil servant from Palopo, observes:

Well, women are good at organizing weddings, but calabai are good too. Maybe calabai are better because they're strong and they can cut up meat and stir mixing bowls. And they are good cooks. And calabai know what hairstyles look good.

Similarly, Ibu Bibi, a relative of Batari, reveals:

If there's to be a wedding, who better to organize it than calabai? Calabai have the strength (*kekuatan*) and endurance (*bisa tahan*) of a man, things that are important for mixing the huge pots of food, and they have the creativity (*kreativitas*) and patience (*kesabaran*) of a woman, which are important in decorating the house and applying makeup.

Because calabai are considered particularly well suited to wedding organization, they are put in charge of a number of important functions, including cooking the wedding food, decorating the places where wedding ceremonies will be held, and dressing and applying makeup to the bride and her retainers. The calabai whom Ibu Tungke' approached to help with Batari and Cakara's wedding was Yulia, a 33-year-old calabai who is a veteran of many weddings. Yulia recalls hir initial meeting with Ibu Tungke':

Two weeks ago, when Ibu Tungke''s family came to see me, we wrote up the wedding agenda (*acara pernikahan*). Then I was given enough money to buy ingredients to cook all the wedding food. You know

I like prices are so cheap.

FIGURE 7.4   Wedding cake made by calabai

what? I have to make 10 kilograms of cake (*kue*)! There are two types of cake that need to be made. There's dry cake (*kue kering*) and moist cake (*kue basah*) (Figure 7.4). All these cakes will cost around Rp70,000 (US$7), and I also have to make other food, and all of that will cost another Rp70,000, food like rice, meat, vegetables, soup. And then there are the decorations (*hiasan*) and clothing and accessories for the bridal party. And the bridal platform. This comes to about Rp300,000 (US$30). We calabai have to decorate the house and bedroom about three days before the wedding. For one wedding there's usually three calabai, so for this wedding I will have two calabai helping me.

One of the calabai helping Yulia organize Batari and Cakara's wedding is Ndari, a 30-year-old calabai. Ndari talks generally about hir role in weddings, with some specific mention of Batari and Cakara's:

The busiest months for weddings, and for me, are two months before and two months after Ramadan [the Islamic fasting month]. Then everyone wants to get married! Have mercy (*Ya Ampun*)! Usually people, like Batari's family, come one month before the wedding and we sort things out. They tell me how many people they will invite. Usually this is between 500 and 1000. Then we work out how much food is needed and then we all go together to the market. So Batari's family came one month before the wedding—usually it's the parents of the bride who come—and then we went to the market. Often I am so busy people have to queue! Ten days before Batari's wedding we will start preparing. We will do the cooking at the bride's house; that's how it usually is, but it's changing. Usually the bride and groom have separate wedding ceremonies; the groom's is a week after the bride's. I often do both. Sometimes calabai cook at their own house and take food to the bride's house. Sometimes, too, when there are lots of weddings, I have my apprentices (*anak buah*) go and work at weddings as well; then I am like the boss.

Yulia and Ndari both detailed the types of work that they will be required to undertake at Batari and Cakara's wedding. The most important task calabai are responsible for is the preparation of the wedding food. As Yulia and Ndari note, sometime before the wedding they went to the market with Batari's family to start purchasing the food stuffs that will be needed for the wedding festivities. Then around three days before the wedding, a number of calabai met at Ibu Tungke's house to begin cooking the vast quantities of food required, as the following excerpt from my field notes reveals:

> *I went to Yulia's this morning and hir neighbors told me s/he was already at Ibu Tungke's house. When I arrived there, I found Yulia and Ndari in the kitchen along with ten other calabai making food for Batari and Cakara's wedding. While Yulia said s/he had two other calabai helping, for the cooking part it always seems like everyone comes to help, and for good reason too, as there is so much to be done. Tomorrow a buffalo will be slaughtered and cooked along with other main courses. When I arrived, Yulia was mixing eggs, flour, sugar, and water into a large bowl. S/he kept adding more flour, or more water, trying to get the mixture just right. When the mixture was the right consistency, Yulia passed the bowl down to the next calabai, who took a plastic whisk and beat the mixture until it was light and fluffy. The next calabai in line then took the bowl and poured the mixture into a tin. The tin was then placed into the oven, which was a letterbox-sized contraption with a kerosene flame below. After eight minutes or so, it was pulled out, inverted, and reinserted. After this process, the next calabai applied icing to the cake and the final calabai in line painted floral decorations on it. There were a few women helping with the decoration part, but they were continually teased because, as even they admitted, their creations lacked the skill of those decorated by calabai. Indeed, Yulia made the following light-hearted comment:*

It's good when we all work together, but Ibu Nur just doesn't have the touch, do you dear (*sayang*)? When she is finished, I always have to patch it up! Look, see how the icing is running outside the outline? She just doesn't have the patience!

The cooking of food is one of the most time-consuming roles calabai undertake at weddings. During preparations for Batari and Cakara's wedding, I had the opportunity to talk with many of the calabai involved. In the following conversation, Andi Dian, a calabai in her 60s who also worked at Batari's cousin's wedding, reveals what is involved in being an *Indo' Botting*:

AUTHOR: Why are calabai the ones who are asked to organize (*mengurus*) weddings?

ANDI DIAN: I don't know [chuckle]. Maybe they're smarter! But women are good cooks too, and good at organizing. Sometimes women are chosen. In fact, one of my apprentices (*anak buah*) is a woman.

AUTHOR: So people learn to become *Indo' Botting* from a *guru*, like you?

ANDI DIAN: Yeah, but some go to Jakarta, there's a school there. I actually went to Jakarta and studied there to become an *Indo' Botting*, but I had a *guru* here too.

AUTHOR: So how did you become an *Indo' Botting*?

ANDI DIAN: I was called by one of the leaders because s/he thought I had talent, and so I went and worked for hir and became hir *anak buah*.

AUTHOR: Is most of your work around here in Sengkang?

ANDI DIAN: No, actually I am very often called to go to Makassar to organize weddings, and more than once I've been called to Jakarta. You see, lots of Bugis people have moved around the place: they like to travel (*massompe'*, B). So, if there's a Bugis person in Jakarta who wants to get married, then they will definitely want Bugis food, and they will want to have someone come who can make good Bugis food, so I am called to go to Jakarta. I am paid an average fee of about Rp1 million (US$100), a bit more if it's a rich family. They also pay for my round trip. It's also very important if there's a Bugis wedding to have a special kind of cake called *béppa toriolo* (B, "cake of the people of the olden days"). Sometimes it's called *béppa puté* (B, white cake). It's a very old and sacred type of cake. The basic ingredients include flour, water, eggs, and sugar. When it's mixed, it's made into a cone shape and then it becomes brittle [it resembles thick, dried pastry]. This must be present at any Bugis wedding, like calabai, right! If it's not made, then there will be bad luck and disaster, and the marriage will not be successful, if it even lasts very long at all. Because no one in Jakarta knows how to make it, you have to get someone who can.

AUTHOR: Like you?

ANDI DIAN: Right! Lots of *waria* don't know how to make it. The Rp1 million I am paid includes the cost of making the food and hiring the special

wedding clothes, and also the decorations and the makeup. But I
have to admit, I am already old. I now usually leave the makeup
to one of my young *anak buah* because they are better at those
things.

In addition to cooking, Andi Dian highlights a number of other important
roles that calabai undertake at weddings, including decorating the areas that
will be used for wedding celebrations. Indeed, two days before Batari and
Cakara's wedding, Yulia, Ndari, and a number of other calabai went to Batari's
house and started decorating. Yulia outlines what had to be achieved:

Well, it's like this, Serli (Sharyn). The wedding is in two days' time and
we have to get the tent put up, but of course we always have men for
that! Then when that is put up we have to put up the decorations (*hiasan*)
and the wedding platform. So there's pretty cloth and wall hangings
and this all makes the inside look beautiful. We have to arrange all the
chairs and work out where everyone is going to sit. We have to make
sure the kitchen is set up out the back for all the cooking that will take
place on the day.

With the cooking preparations well under way and the decorations complete,
the next task Yulia and Ndari had to undertake was getting Batari ready for the
wedding. On the morning of the actual marriage ceremony, Yulia and Ndari
arrived early at Batari's house. Ndari speaks more of what took place:

We calabai are specialists in hair and makeup. So we are here because we
have to set Batari's hair. You've seen Bugis brides, haven't you? They
have markings on their forehead [black lines that are drawn to give the
effect of wavy hair] and a lot of jewelry has to be put in their hair, and
they have to make their face white with powder and their clothes have to
be just right. Calabai are experts in this; a bride could never do it on her
own (Figure 7.5).

Helping the bride get ready reflects the intimate access that calabai have to
brides. This close relationship is reflected in the term of endearment and authority used to refer to calabai, *Indo' Botting* (Figure 7.6). As we waited for Batari to
finish bathing, I asked Ndari why calabai are referred to as *Indo' Botting*:

It's like this. *Indo' Botting* do the hair and the makeup of the bride; they
do everything like a mother (*indo'*, B) would. So it's like they are the
mother of the bride. Because the bride is put into seclusion (*dipingit*)
before the wedding, *Indo' Botting* have to take everything to her and take
care of her. *Indo' Botting* are exactly like younger sisters (*adik perempuan*).
The Raja chooses a calabai to help the bride because s/he isn't a man and
s/he is very creative and good at doing things. In the palace there is a
place called *keputren* . . . that's like a women's room . . . and only the
Queen and her daughters and *Indo' Botting* are allowed to enter. The
Indo' Botting is allowed to enter because s/he is calabai.

FIGURE 7.5 A bride who was dressed and made-up by calabai

FIGURE 7.6 Two calabai *Indo' Botting* flanking a newly married couple

At this point I asked about the possibility of an *Indo' Botting* lying about being calabai just to get close to the princess to watch her bathe. Ndari replied, "Oh no, that wouldn't happen, no one would ever be brave enough to lie to the Raja because if they were found out they would be killed."

Similar sentiments of *Indo' Botting* helping the bride are noted by Andi Muhammad, a local Sengkang man, "If the Raja wanted to marry, he would adopt a calabai as a daughter so that the future bride would have a sister to help her get ready for the wedding."

Both of these narratives stress the link between nobility and *Indo' Botting*. While traditionally calabai may have almost exclusively assisted in the weddings of nobles, this has changed. Calabai now frequently work at weddings for low-status people, such as Batari and Cakara. One of the reasons for this shift is due to the official disbanding of the royal courts, which meant that the nobility could no longer adequately support calabai activities, forcing calabai to look for other business opportunities. Moreover, ordinary people have begun to lay claim to traditions that were once the sole preserve of the noble class.

Once Yulia and Ndari were satisfied that Batari and her retainers were appropriately dressed and made-up, the bride was able to begin attending the many wedding ceremonies. While various smaller ceremonies were scattered throughout the week, keeping calabai busy, it was on the final day that the most elaborate ceremonies were held. This included the official marriage ceremony where Batari and Cakara were officially wed. While calabai continually prepared food, checked that the decorations stayed as they should, and made sure that Batari always looked her best, on the final night of the wedding celebrations they had another role to perform. At the reception, calabai were responsible for much of the practical arrangements, as outlined in my field notes:

> *Today was the final day of the wedding and the very last event was the reception* (resepsi). *It involved the wedding couple sitting in state, and they were greeted in turn by all of the guests. While the cooking, costumes, and decorations were complete, Yulia and Ndari's work was still not over. They and a number of other calabai were often being called upon to resolve different problems. Yulia appeared to enjoy giving orders. When the groom arrived with his 500-person entourage, it was calabai who arranged the procession. For instance, Yulia and Ndari had to state which guests should enter through which door, who should immediately follow the groom, where the greeting party should stand, how many people should go into the bride's bedroom, and who should carry what gift. When everyone had arrived and was seated, the buffet dinner was brought out. The food was really good. Shortly after everyone had finished eating, the evening's entertainment began. While a band had been hired, without a doubt the event that caused most merriment was* wardut, *calabai performing karaoke. It was a great lot of fun. Singing and dancing went on until past midnight, but at 10 p.m. the newlyweds retired to their elaborately decorated bridal chamber.*

With this, Batari and Cakara's wedding came to a successful close. By describing their wedding, I hope that the central roles calabai play in this and many other Bugis weddings have been established. Before finishing this section, however,

I would like to make a brief comment on social attitudes toward calabai with respect to weddings. While most people acknowledge the benefits of employing calabai to organize weddings, negative attitudes are expressed, as the following excerpt from my field notes reveals:

> *I went to a wedding in Paré Paré yesterday. When I asked if calabai had made the cakes and set up the decorations, the father looked quite astonished and said emphatically, "No! Women did that." It is the first time I have felt embarrassed asking that question. While some people don't employ calabai, the usual reason given is that all calabai were already booked out or that the family cannot afford to hire calabai because they cost more than women—it is said that calabai have particular skills in respect to wedding organization that women don't have and thus they can demand a higher price. The father also told me that although they live in Paré Paré, a Bugis area, they are not originally from there, and they haven't adopted all of the customs of the area. He said that his customs are a mix of Javanese and Arab customs. Talking with him I got the sense that he thought calabai were unsophisticated and strange. He said hiring calabai was not modern* (tak maju) *and not something good.* (Field notes, 2000)

In another instance, I attended a wedding in Soppeng where no calabai were employed. When I spoke to the bride's grandfather, he told me, "It's not good to have calabai. We're Muslim, and it's women's work to cook. No, it's not good to have calabai, they are not doing right with God, and it's no good to have them at weddings."

I include these two examples to indicate that although calabai have a recognized role in many Bugis weddings, not everyone is supportive of this role. A strictly religious wedding does not necessarily mean, however, that calabai will not be present:

> *I went with my host-family to a wedding near Soppeng today. We had to walk a kilometer from the road to reach the house. Perhaps the most interesting aspect of this wedding was the central role of Islam. There were four formal speeches. During one of these speeches the bride's father even thanked me in English for coming: "Tank you Miz Serli for your coming." All these speeches started with an extensive Islamic recitation. A woman also melodiously recited the Qur'an for thirty minutes. Calabai were very evident in their role of cooking and seating people correctly.* (Field notes, 2000)

There are, then, different opinions about employing calabai to oversee marriage celebrations. While some people are openly hostile to the idea of calabai and their role in Bugis weddings, many people recognize calabai as having a constructive role in organizing and managing Bugis weddings, even if these people do not seek their services. Because of their particular constitution, which is considered to combine male and female attributes, calabai are believed to be especially adept at cooking wedding food, decorating areas that will host wedding ceremonies, and making the bride and her retinue look beautiful. These roles help provide calabai with a legitimate position in Bugis society.

CONCLUSION

As a way of exploring the identities of bissu and calabai, I selected Bugis weddings as a site for examination. Weddings are the most celebrated life-cycle ritual among Bugis, and bissu and calabai are key players in the celebrations attached to them. The chapter was divided into two sections, each section describing a wedding using data presented in the form of my own field notes and the narratives of informants. My aim in this chapter has been to contribute to the ethnography on multiple genders among Bugis. My particular focus has been the place of bissu and calabai in wedding rituals and practices.

In the first section, I detailed the marriage of Andi Marawah and Bambang. In this high-status wedding, bissu undertook a number of important roles. Mariani and Haji Baco', both bissu, offered advice on the correct way to carry out an assortment of traditional customs. The pair also contacted the spirit world, reaffirming the link between the wedding couple and their heavenly origins. Mariani and Haji Baco' sought blessings from *dewata* to ensure that the wedding would be a success and that Andi Marawah and Bambang would have a long and prosperous life together. This wedding revealed the important roles bissu often undertake in contemporary high-status Bugis weddings.

In the second section, I detailed the marriage of Batari and Cakara. In this wedding, calabai played many crucial roles and were largely responsible for executing a successful commoner Bugis wedding. As a way of examining this, I followed the experiences of Yulia and Ndari, both calabai, and revealed the variety of roles they assumed at this wedding, and at weddings in general. The most important of these roles include cooking the wedding food, decorating areas used for wedding celebrations, and ensuring that the bride and her retinue are beautifully dressed.

There are a number of reasons why bissu and calabai play central roles in weddings. In the mythological past, bissu facilitated the first earthly marriage between Wé Nyili' Timo and Batara Guru. The power of bissu to bring about this union resulted in bissu being considered embodiments of auspicious power. Bissu, and by extension calabai, assert this past role to legitimize their contemporary position. Another reason for the prominent role of bissu and calabai in weddings, which ties into this former reason, relates to issues of status. Bissu are believed to have descended to earth with the first white-blooded rulers. In high-status weddings, bissu reaffirm the connection of the nobles to their heavenly origins. In this respect, the role of bissu reveals a moment of connection where androgynous beings are most efficacious in facilitating the uniting of the spirit world and white-blooded descendents. The employment of bissu visibly reproduces the high status of nobles. Calabai originally assisted in the wedding celebrations of royalty and the nobility, and they too can tap into this heritage to assert contemporary legitimacy. The employment of strategies connecting them to the past is thus one way in which bissu and calabai maintain a position in Bugis society.

The embodiment of male and female elements is another reason why bissu and calabai are sought after as wedding officiates. Before a high-status wedding can go ahead, *dewata* have to be contacted. The permission of *dewata* must be sought to sanctify the marriage, and a blessing from *dewata* must be bestowed upon the bride and groom. The only individuals able to contact the spirit world are bissu. It is the combination of male and female elements contained within bissu embodiment that enables them to mediate with *dewata* and be conduits of blessings from *dewata*. The nature of calabai, which is also seen as a combination of male and female elements, means that calabai can tap into this discourse of power attributed to androgyny. Moreover, the particular constitution of calabai is believed by many to make them perfectly suited to wedding organization: Calabai are strong and enduring like men, and creative and patient like women.

A further reason why bissu and calabai have such a visible role in Bugis weddings relates to current efforts to revitalize Bugis *adat*. Both bissu and calabai are recognized by many Bugis as experts in traditional customs and practices. As such, both are sought after to offer advice on how things ought to be performed. In efforts to mobilize the reconstruction of *adat* and assert ethnic identity, bissu and calabai have been seen as effective means of achieving this. Moreover, bissu and calabai have positioned themselves as the most qualified individuals to achieve these objectives. In affirming and reinforcing the importance of *adat*, bissu and calabai assert their central role in Bugis society. Weddings, then, provide bissu and calabai not only with a way of making a living but with the opportunity to occupy a recognized position in contemporary Bugis society.

8

Conclusion: Five Genders

This case study has used ethnographic material to illuminate how some Bugis think about and experience gender. More specifically, the case study has examined the subjectivities of five variously gendered identities: *makkunrai* (B, women), *oroané* (B, men), calalai, calabai, and bissu. The two former categories reflect normative Bugis gender ideals, and these were explored primarily in Chapter 3 in order to contextualize the setting in which the other identities are formed. The book focused primarily on the latter three, however, because these identities challenge gender norms and allow for a more rigorous analysis of the complexities of gender.

In order to examine Bugis gender and Bugis gender identities, the book was divided into two parts. The first part consisted of an introductory chapter and two chapters that established the more contextual foundations of the book. The second part consisted of four ethnographic chapters. Chapter 2 was dedicated to presenting an understanding of Bugis notions of gender. This chapter showed that gender in Bugis South Sulawesi is thought by many to be constituted through a range of factors, such as sexuality, biology, and subjectivity. These factors are often complementary, rather than oppositional, but they do not necessarily always work in harmony. Chapter 2 demonstrated how these various factors combine in the formation of gender identity, and it developed an understanding of what is often meant by the term *gender* in Bugis South Sulawesi. This particular understanding of gender allows conceptual space for five gendered categories.

Having examined how gender can be understood in Bugis South Sulawesi, I moved on to ask the fundamental question, "Is gender an important consideration in everyday Bugis life?" In many published sources on South Sulawesi, gender is downplayed as a key organizational concept. In Chapter 3, however, I suggested that gender is of central importance in the organization and practice of Bugis

FIGURE 8.1   The author with her two host-nieces, Cici (left) and Nabilah (right)

social life and that an understanding of gender is necessary in order to appreciate other aspects of Bugis culture. The concepts of *siri'* (B, shame/honor) and social status underpin Bugis society. Yet without an awareness of gender, it would be impossible to see how gender considerations mediate these concepts. Through an analysis of notions of *siri'* and social status, and government and Islamic discourses, it became evident that there are very clear notions of what constitutes ideal Bugis gender types. The purpose of this chapter was thus twofold: to highlight the centrality and importance of gender in Bugis society, and to examine processes of gendering by revealing gender ideals.

The second part of the book consisted of four ethnographic chapters. Chapter 4 focused on females who neither want nor aspire to be women or men. Rather, calalai present identities that differ from normative gender expectations. It is in identity formation that the particular understanding of Bugis gender is central. Because gender is not thought to be determined by biological sex alone, calalai can be seen as other than women, and in some respects, this allows certain degrees of freedom (e.g., to perform masculinity). However, biological sex is important in the sense that it limits the possibilities of gender identity; for instance, the fact that calalai are female is never forgotten and there is continual pressure placed on most calalai to marry and have children, particularly until calalai are in their late 30s. I also discussed calalai masculinity and examined ways in which calalai both conform to and challenge normative gender models.

In Chapter 5, I explored the identities of feminine males, or calabai. This chapter was divided into four sections. In the first section, I examined notions of ideal masculinity. In the second section, I showed how some males feel at odds with dominant images of masculinity. Because calabai tend to reject norms of masculinity, many calabai model their identities to an extent on a mix of local, national, and Western images of femininity. Calabai generally do not aim to be or become women, though, and in the third section, I looked at ways in which calabai differentiate themselves from women. The fourth section included a discussion of societal responses to calabai, showing that although national and Islamic discourses may officially oppose calabai identity, the latter's role as *Indo' Botting* (B, Wedding Mothers) and the particular understanding of gender in Bugis South Sulawesi, which makes room for gender variance, mean that calabai are generally tolerated and even accepted within Bugis society. I concluded by suggesting that while, in certain respects, calabai embody a form of femininity, they assert and occupy a distinct gendered place in Bugis society.

Chapter 6 concentrated on bissu shamans. While providing insights into bissu subjectivity, this chapter also explored ways in which gender considerations underpin bissu identity. Bissu are considered to derive their power from the notion that they are predifferentiated beings who embody a perfect combination of female and male elements; this androgyny is enriched through material accoutrements, such as flowers and *keris*. This union of female and male also enables bissu to mediate with the spirit world. Bissu embody feminine and masculine elements, and this is considered to render them spiritually powerful. The fundamental importance of gender in Bugis society is thus revealed in part through bissu subjectivity.

Bugis weddings were the focus of Chapter 7. Such events are excellent sites to examine, as weddings reveal a great deal about the respective roles of bissu and calabai. Bugis weddings also bring to light notions of gender. In the first section, I recounted a high-status wedding in Jakarta at which bissu officiated. This wedding clearly showed the important position of bissu in high-status weddings and outlined the functions bissu perform. The second section detailed a commoner wedding in Sengkang at which calabai played central roles. Many weddings in Sengkang are organized to some extent by calabai. I thus examined the responsibility of calabai in cooking wedding food, preparing costumes, doing hair and makeup, and general wedding organization. By recounting these two weddings, it became clear that both bissu and calabai continue to undertake recognized roles in Bugis society.

Not too long before I finished my main fieldwork, I was privileged to meet a man of great insight. He not only spent many hours talking with me about Bugis culture but he also introduced me to many *adat* experts. Perhaps peculiarly, one of the qualities of Pak Mansur that I most admired was his irreverence. While he often unwittingly made me feel uncomfortable, he always challenged me intellectually. Pak Mansur is in his mid-40s, and he is married with two small children. While he was only formally educated until the age of 16, he has managed to secure a respected government position. During one of our final conversations, Pak Mansur asked probing questions about the future implications and benefits of my work. In doing this, he made me think about the larger potential impact of my research. This is what Pak Mansur said:

> I'm sorry, Serli [Sharyn], but is it okay if I am a bit, um, critical of, you
> know, research like, um, like of your research? Is it okay? [I nod] We
> are, after all, in the new era of free speech, we aren't under Suharto and
> his silences anymore, right? Well, it's all very well that you're here and
> you're studying the roles and the functions of calabai, but there are many
> bigger issues at stake here, right, like their lack of political rights (*hak
> politik*) and their lack of legal rights (*hak hukum*). *Waria* (a national
> subjectivity similar to calabai) are, after all, citizens of this country (*warga
> negara*), right? What we need to do is to set up some sort of official
> organization so they can get together and voice their problems, and so
> they can get together to develop policy. It's good that you're doing
> research on calabai because up until now no one has thought calabai
> were important enough to do research on. It's very important. But what
> happens after you go? You will take all the benefits and what will be left?
> I know your research is for S3 (PhD), but wouldn't it be great if your
> legacy was more than Dr. in front of your name? If you want, we can
> start developing a policy and take it to the Bupati (Regent) to get his
> support, and we can approach the DPR (House of Representatives) in
> Jakarta. Our aim could include getting a Department of Waria Affairs or
> a broader category of gender affairs that deals with categories falling
> outside men and women. In this way, calabai can get their problems
> addressed, and they will have a way to deal with discrimination. Calabai
> need to be able to protect their human rights, don't they? We can get
> calabai into government and they can protect the rights of other calabai.
> Maybe we can get some models from more advanced (*maju*) countries,
> like Australia, yeah? We also need to get a definition of their social roles
> and functions, and, more importantly, we must define their gender.
> Calabai are rather closed off (*tertutup*) at the moment, and we need to
> help them open doors. We can look at people's perception of calabai,
> what their prejudices are. If I am in the mosque and I hear the *ulama*
> (Islamic leader) preaching about the danger of HIV/AIDS and he says
> that AIDS is caused by *waria* and being spread only by *waria,* well, I know

this isn't true; in fact, if you look at the statistics, you will see that *waria* make up a very small percentage of those people with AIDS in Makassar, but if you had no other information, of course you would believe the *ulama,* right? We need to address problems of false education. So there should be a greater aim here than just a Dr., because your work has more potential than just a title. Oh, but I hope that I haven't offended you. I didn't mean to, I just thought it was important to say.

Pak Mansur's comments made me really think about the potential of my research. Could I really just complete my analysis of Bugis gender and submit my PhD, knowing that maybe only half a dozen people would read it? It seemed a shame to limit the potential audience considering that so many people had invested such a large amount of their time sharing with me their thoughts on gender. A motivation for writing this ethnographic case study, then, comes from the hope of increasing awareness of the subjectivities of not only calabai but also of calalai and bissu. I hope Pak Mansur is pleased with this first step.

References

Acciaioli, G. (1989). *Searching for Good Fortune: The Making of a Bugis Shore Community at Lake Lindu, Central Sulawesi.* Unpublished PhD, The Australian National University, Canberra.

Ahmed, L. (1992). *Women and Gender in Islam: Historical Roots of a Modern Debate.* New Haven, CT: Yale University Press.

Andaya, L. (1981). *The Heritage of Arung Palakka: A History of South Sulawesi (Celebes) in the Seventeenth Century.* The Hague: Martinus Nijhoff.

Andaya, L. (2000). The Bissu: Study of a Third Gender in Indonesia. In B. W. Andaya (Ed.), *Other Pasts: Women, Gender, and History in Early Modern Southeast Asia* (pp. 27–46). Honolulu: The University of Hawai'i Press.

Badaruddin, M. (1980). *Bissu dan Peralatannya (Bissu and their Paraphernalia).* Ujung Pandang: Proyek Pengembangan Permuseuman Sulawesi Selatan (Project for Restoring South Sulawesi's Museums).

Bateson, G., & Mead, M. (1942). *Balinese Character: A Photographic Analysis* (Vol. 2). New York: New York Academy of Sciences.

Bennett, L. (2002). Modernity, Desire and Courtship. In L. Manderson & P. Liamputtong (Eds.), *Coming of Age in South and Southeast Asia* (pp. 96–112). Richmond, UK: Curzon Press.

Bennett, L. R. (2004). *Women, Islam and Modernity: Single Women, Sexuality and Reproductive Health in Contemporary Indonesia.* London: Routledge Curzon.

Blackwood, E. (1995). Senior Women, Model Mothers, and Dutiful Wives: Managing Gender Contradictions in a Minangkabau Village. In A. Ong & M. Peletz (Eds.), *Bewitching Women, Pious Men: Gender and Body Politics in Southeast Asia* (pp. 124–158). Berkeley: University of California Press.

Blackwood, E. (1998). *Tombois* in West Sumatra: Constructing Masculinity and Erotic Desire. *Cultural Anthropology, 13*(4), 491–521.

Blair, L., & Blair, L. (1988). *Ring of Fire.* London: Bantam.

Boellstorff, T. (2004). The Emergence of Political Homophobia in Indonesia. *Ethnos: Journal of Anthropology, 69*(4), 465–486.

Boellstorff, T. (2005). *The Gay Archipelago: Sexuality and Nation in Indonesia.* Princeton: Princeton University Press.

Boellstorff, T., & Lindquist, J. (2004). Bodies of Emotion: Rethinking Culture and Emotion through Southeast Asia. *Ethnos: Journal of Anthropology, 69*(4), 437–444.

Bolin, A. (1994). Transcending and Transgendering: Male-to-Female Transsexuals, Dichotomy, and Diversity. In G. Herdt (Ed.), *Third Sex, Third Gender: Beyond Sexual Dimorphism in Culture and History* (pp. 447–485). New York: Zone Books.

Brenner, S. (1996). Reconstructing Self and Society: Javanese Muslim Women and the Veil. *American Ethnologist, 23*(4), 673–697.

Brenner, S. (1998). *The Domestication of Desire: Women, Wealth, and Modernity in Java.* Princeton, NJ: Princeton University Press.

Brenner, S. A. (1995). Why Women Rule the Roost: Rethinking Javanese Ideologies of Gender and Self-Control. In A. Ong & M. G. Peletz (Eds.), *Bewitching Women, Pious Men: Gender and Body Politics in Southeast Asia* (pp. 19–50). Berkeley: University of California Press.

Brooke, J. (1848). *Narratives of Events in Borneo and Celebes.* London: Murry.

Butler, J. (1990). *Gender Trouble: Feminism and the Subversion of Identity.* New York: Routledge.

Butler, J. (1993). *Bodies That Matter: On the Discursive Limits of "Sex."* New York: Routledge.

Caldwell, I. (1988). *South Sulawesi AD 1300–1600: Ten Bugis Texts.* Unpublished PhD, Australian National University, Canberra.

Chabot, H. T. (1996). *Kinship, Status, and Gender in South Celebes.* Leiden, The Netherlands: Koninklijk Instituut voor de Taal-, Land- en Volkenkunde (KITLV) Press. Original publication in 1950.

Collins, E., & Bahar, E. (2000). To Know Shame: Malu and Its Uses in Malay Societies. *Crossroads: An Interdisciplinary Journal of Southeast Asian Studies, 14*(1), 35–69.

Crawfurd, J. (1820). *History of the Indian Archipelago: Containing an Account of the Manners, Arts, Languages, Religions, Institutions, and Commerce of its Inhabitants* (Vol. 3). Edinburgh, UK: Archibal Constable and Co.

Cummings, W. (2002). *Making Blood White: Historical Transformations in Early Modern Makassar.* Honolulu: The University of Hawai'i Press.

Davies, S. G. (2006[a]). Gender and Status in Bugis Society. In S. Epstein (Ed.), *Understanding Indonesia* (pp. 93–106). Wellington, New Zealand: Victoria University of Wellington Press.

Davies, S. G. (2006[b]). Thinking of Gender in a Holistic Sense: Understandings of Gender in Sulawesi, Indonesia. In V. Demos & M. T. Segal (Eds.), *Gender and the Local-Global Nexus: Theory, Research, and Action* (Vol. 10, pp. 1–24). Oxford: Elsevier.

Davies, S. G. (forthcoming[a]). *Gender Diversity in Indonesia: Beyond Gender Binaries.* London: Routledge Curzon.

Davies, S. G. (forthcoming[b]). Hunting Down Love: Female Masculinity in Bugis Society. In E. Blackwood & S. Wieringa (Eds.), *Women's Same-Sex Experiences in a Globalizing Asia.* New York: Palgrave Macmillan.

de Beauvoir, S. (1947). *The Second Sex.* New York: Knopf.

Douglas, H., & Wellenkamp, J. (1994). *Contentment and Suffering: Culture and Experience in Toraja.* New York: Columbia University Press.

Errington, S. (1989). *Meaning and Power in a Southeast Asian Realm.* Princeton, NJ: Princeton University Press.

Foucault, M. (1977). *Discipline and Punish: The Birth of the Prison* (A. Sheridan, Trans.). Harmondsworth, UK: Penguin.

Gayatri, B. J. D. (1995). Indonesian Lesbians Writing Their Own Script: Issues of Feminism and Sexuality. In M. Reinfelder (Ed.), *From Amazon to Zami: Towards a Global Lesbian Feminism* (pp. 86–98). London: Cassell.

Geertz, C. (1973a). Deep Play: Notes on the Balinese Cockfight. In C. Geertz (Ed.), *The Interpretation of Cultures: Selected Essays* (pp. 412–453). New York: Basic Books.

Geertz, C. (1973b). Person, Time and Conduct in Bali. In C. Geertz (Ed.), *The Interpretation of Cultures: Selected Essays* (pp. 360–411). New York: Basic Books.

Geertz, C. (1976). *The Religion of Java*. Chicago: University of Chicago Press.

Geertz, H. (1968). Latah in Java: A Theoretical Paradox. *Psychiatry, 22,* 225–237.

Gervaise, N. (1971). *Historical Description of the Kingdom of Macasar in the East-Indies.* Westmead: Gregg International Publishers, originally published in 1701.

Good, B. (2004). Rethinking "Emotions" in Southeast Asia. *Ethnos: Journal of Anthropology, 69*(4), 529–533.

Graham, S. (2001a). Negotiating Gender: *Calalai'* in Bugis Society. *Intersections: Gender, History, and Culture in the Asian Context, 6*(August), available at http://wwwsshe.murdoch.edu.au/intersections/issue6/graham.html.

Graham, S. (2001b). Sulawesi's Fifth Gender. *Inside Indonesia, April–June* (66), 16–17.

Graham, S. (2003). Bissu dalam La Galigo (Bissu in La Galigo). In N. Rahman (Ed.), *La Galigo: Menelusuri Jejak Warisan Sastra Dunia (La Galigo: Investigating the Legacy of World Literature)* (pp. 499–515). Makassar: Pusat Studi La Galigo, Divisi Ilmu Sosial dan Humaniora, Pusat Kegiatan Penelitian Universitas Hasanuddin dengan Permerintah Kabupaten Barru (La Galigo Study Center, Faculty of Social Science, University Hasanuddin, and the Barru Provincial Government).

Graham, S. (2004a). *Hunters, Wedding Mothers and Androgynous Priests: Conceptualising Gender amongst Bugis in South Sulawesi, Indonesia.* Unpublished PhD dissertation, University of Western Australia, Perth.

Graham, S. (2004b). It's Like One of Those Puzzles: Conceptualising Gender among Bugis. *Journal of Gender Studies, 13*(2), 107–116.

Graham, S. (2004c). While Diving, Drink Water: Bisexual and Transgender Intersections in South Sulawesi, Indonesia. *Journal of Bisexuality, 3*(3/4), 231–248.

Hamonic, G. (1975). Travestissement et Bisexualité chez Les Bissu du Pays Bugis. *Archipel, 10,* 153–157.

Hamonic, G. (1977a). Les "Fausses-Femmes" du Pays Bugis (Celebes-Sud). *Objects et Mondes, 17,* 39–46.

Hamonic, G. (1977b). Pengantar Studi Perbandingan Kosmogoni Sulawesi Selatan: Tentang Naskah Asal-usul Dewata-dewata Bugis yang Belum Pernah Diterbitkan (An Introductory Comparative Study of South Sulawesi Cosmology: A Never-Before Published Manuscript that Originates from the Bugis Spirit World). *Citra Masyarakat Indonesia: Rangkuman bererapa dari Peneliti Barat,* 13–79.

Hamonic, G. (1980). Mallawolo: Chants Bugis pour la Sacralisation des Anciens Princes de Célèbes-Sud. Textes et Traductions. *Archipel, 19,* 43–79.

Hamonic, G. (1987a). *Kepercayaan Pra-Islam di Sulawesi Selatan Berdasarkan Lagu-lagu Suci dan Pujaan Pendeta Bissu (Pre-Islamic Beliefs of South Sulawesi Based on the Sacred Songs and Worship of Bissu Priests).* Paper presented at the Second International

Koninklijk Instituut voor de Taal-, Land- en Volkenkunde (KITLV) Workshop on Indonesian Studies: Trade, Society and Belief in South Sulawesi and its Maritime World, Leiden.

Hamonic, G. (1987b). *Le Langage Des Dieux: Cultes et Pouvoirs Pre-Islamiques en Pays Bugis Celebes-Sud Indonesie.* Paris: Edition du Centre National de la Recherche Scientifique.

Hamonic, G. (1988). En Quete des Dieux Bugis: Entre Mythe et Rituel, Entre Silence et Parole (In Quest of Bugis Gods: Between Myth and Ritual, Silence and Speech). *Revue de l'Histoire des Religions, 205*(4), 345–366.

Hamonic, G. (2002). *Kepercayaan dan Upacara dari Budaya Bugis Kuno: Pujaan Pendeta Bissu dalam Mitos La Galigo (Beliefs and Rituals in Proto-Historical Bugis Culture: The Worship of Bissu Priests in La Galigo Mythology).* Paper presented at the Festival dan Seminar Internasional La Galigo (The International La Galigo Festival and Seminar), Pancana, Sulawesi Selatan, Indonesia.

Harvey, B. (1978). *Tradition, Islam, and Rebellion: South Sulawesi 1950–1965.* Unpublished PhD, Cornell University, Ithaca, New York.

Heider, K. (1991). *Landscapes of Emotion: Mapping Three Cultures of Emotion in Indonesia.* Cambridge, UK: Cambridge University Press.

Herdt, G. (Ed.). (1994). *Third Sex, Third Gender: Beyond Sexual Dimorphism in Culture and History.* New York: Zone Books.

Herdt, G. (1994). Third Sexes and Third Genders. In G. Herdt (Ed.), *Third Sex, Third Gender: Beyond Sexual Dimorphism in Culture and History* (pp. 21–84). New York: Zone Books.

Holt, C. (1939). *Dance Quest in Celebes.* Paris: Les Archives Internationales de la Dance.

Idrus, N. I. (2003). *"To Take Each Other": Bugis Practices of Gender, Sexuality and Marriage.* Unpublished PhD, Australian National University, Canberra.

Idrus, N. I. (2004). Behind the Notion of *Siala*: Marriage, *Adat* and Islam among the Bugis in South Sulawesi. *Intersections: Gender, History and Culture in the Asian Context, 10*(August), available at http://wwwsshe.murdoch.edu.au/intersections/issue10/idrus.html.

Idrus, N. I., & Bennett, L. (2003). Presumed Consent and Marital Violence in Bugis Society. In L. Manderson & L. Bennett (Eds.), *Violence against Women in Asian Societies* (pp. 30–57). New York: Curzon Press.

Jensen, G., & Suryani, L. K. (1992). *The Balinese People: A Reinvestigation of Character.* Singapore: Oxford University Press.

Jones, C. (2004). Whose Stress? Emotion Work in Middle-Class Javanese Homes. *Ethnos: Journal of Anthropology, 69*(4), 509–528.

Jung, C. (1991). *Wild Swans: Three Daughters of China.* New York: Anchor Books.

Keeler, W. (1983). Shame and Stage Fright in Java. *Ethos, 11*(3), 15–165.

Keeler, W. (1987). *Javanese Shadow Plays, Javanese Selves.* Princeton, NJ: Princeton University Press.

Kennedy, M. (1993). Clothing, Gender, and Ritual Transvestism: The *Bissu* of Sulawesi. *The Journal of Men's Studies, 2*(1), 1–13.

Klima, A. (2004). Thai Love Thai: Financing Emotion in Post-Crash Thailand. *Ethnos: Journal of Anthropology, 69*(4), 445–464.

Koentjaraningrat. (1985). *Javanese Culture.* Singapore: Oxford University Press.

Koolhof, S. (1999). The "La Galigo": A Bugis Encyclopaedia and its Growth. *Bijdragen, Tòt de Taal-, Land- en Volkenkunde, 155*(3), 362–387.

Kulick, D. (1998). *Travesti: Sex, Gender and Culture among Brazilian Transgendered Prostitutes.* Chicago: The University of Chicago.

Lathief, H. (2002). *Bissu: Para Imam yang Menhibur (Bissu: The Entertaining Priests).* Paper presented at the Festival dan Seminar Internasional La Galigo (The International La Galigo Festival and Seminar), Pancana, Sulawesi Selatan, Indonesia.

Lathief, H., Sutton, R. A., & Mohamad, A. M. N. (2001). *Proposal Bantuan Pemugaran Rumah Upacara Bissu: Komunitas Seniman Tradisi Bissu Segeri Pangkep, Sulawesi Selatan (Proposal to Help with the Restoration of the Bissu Ceremony House: Community of Traditional Bissu Artists, Pangkep, South Sulawesi).* Segeri, Indonesia.

Lindquist, J. (2004). Veils and Ecstasy: Negotiating Shame in the Indonesian Borderlands. *Ethnos: Journal of Anthropology, 69*(4), 487–508.

Matthes, B. F. (1872). Over de Bissoe's of Heidensche Priesters en Priesteressen der Boeginezen. *Verhandelingen der Koninklijke Akademie can Wetenschappen, Afdeeling Letterkunde, 17,* 1–50.

Mead, M. (1935). *Sex and Temperament in Three Primitive Societies.* New York: William Morrow.

Mernissi, F. (1991). *The Veil and the Male Elite: A Feminist Interpretation of Women's Rights in Islam* (M. J. Lakeland, Trans. Also published as *Women and Islam: An Historical and Theological Enquiry,* Oxford, Blackwell. ed.). Reading, MA: Addison-Wesley.

Millar, S. (1983). On Interpreting Gender in Bugis Society. *American Ethnologist, 10*(August), 477–493.

Millar, S. (1989). *Bugis Weddings: Rituals of Social Location in Modern Indonesia.* Berkeley: University of California Press.

Nanda, S. (1999). *Neither Man nor Woman: The Hijras of India* (2nd ed.). Boston: Wadsworth.

Nowra, L. (1999). *The Language of the Gods* (Stage Play). Playbox Theatre, Melbourne.

Ortner, S., & Whitehead, H. (Eds.). (1981). *Sexual Meanings: The Cultural Construction of Gender and Sexuality.* Cambridge, UK: Cambridge University Press.

Parker, L. (1992). The Creation of Indonesian Citizens in Balinese Primary Schools. *Review of Indonesian and Malaysian Affairs, 26,* 42–70.

Parker, L. (2002). The Subjectification of Citizenship: Student Interpretations of School Teachings in Bali. *Asian Studies Review, 26*(1), 3–38.

Peletz, M. G. (1996). *Reason and Passion: Representations of Gender in a Malay Society.* Berkeley: University of California Press.

Pelras, C. (1996). *The Bugis.* Oxford, UK: Blackwell Publishers.

Raffles, T. S. (1817). *History of Java.* London: Parbury and Allen.

Ricklefs, M. C. (1993). *A History of Modern Indonesia since c.1300* (2nd ed.). Hong Kong: MacMillan.

Robinson, K. (1998). Forum on Cultural Change. In K. Robinson & M. Paeni (Eds.), *Living through Histories: Culture, History and Social Life in South Sulawesi* (pp. 277–290). Canberra: Department of Anthropology, Research School of Pacific and Asian Studies, Australian National University.

Robinson, K., & Paeni, M. (Eds.). (1998). *Living through Histories: Culture, History and Social Life in South Sulawesi*. Canberra: Department of Anthropology, Research School of Pacific and Asian Studies, Australian National University.

Rosaldo, M. (1983). The Shame of Headhunters and the Autonomy of the Self. *Ethos, 11*(3), 135–151.

Roscoe, W. (1991). *The Zuni Man-Woman*. Albuquerque: University of New Mexico Press.

Roscoe, W. (1998). *Changing Ones: Third and Fourth Genders in Native North America*. New York: St. Martin's Press.

Rossler, M. (2000). From Divine Descent to Administration: Sacred Heirlooms and Political Change in Highland Goa. In R. Tol, K. van Dijk, & G. Acciaioli (Eds.), *Authority and Enterprise among the Peoples of South Sulawesi* (pp. 161–182). Leiden: KITLV Press.

Rottger-Rossler, B. (2000). Shared Responsibility: Some Aspects of Gender and Authority in Makassar Society. In R. Tol, K. van Dijk, & G. Acciaioli (Eds.), *Authority and Enterprise among the Peoples of South Sulawesi* (pp. 143–160). Leiden: KITLV Press.

Silvey, R. (2000a). Diasporic Subjects: Gender and Mobility in South Sulawesi. *Women's Studies International Forum, 23*(4), 501–515.

Silvey, R. (2000b). Stigmatized Spaces: Gender and Mobility under Crisis in South Sulawesi, Indonesia. *Gender Place & Culture: A Journal of Feminist Geography, 7*(2), 143–162.

Sirk, U. (1975). On Old Buginese and Basa Bissu. *Archipel, 10,* 225–237.

Sullivan, N. (1994). *Masters and Managers: A Study of Gender Relations in Urban Java*. St Leonards: Allen and Unwin.

Tol, R., van Dijk, K., & Acciaioli, G. (Eds.). (2000). *Authority and Enterprise among the Peoples of South Sulawesi*. Leiden: KITLV Press.

Tomaszewski, M., Rush, J., & Graham, S. (Writers) (2001). Sex and Priests. In N. Greenaway & H. Oliver (Producer). Sydney: National Geographic.

Trumbach, R. (1994). London's Sapphists: From Three Sexes to Four Genders in the Making of Modern Culture. In G. Herdt (Ed.), *Third Sex, Third Gender: Beyond Sexual Dimorphism in Culture and History* (pp. 111–136). New York: Zone Books.

van der Kroef, J. (1956). Transvestism and the Religious Hermaphrodite. In J. van der Kroef (Ed.), *Indonesia in the Modern World* (Vol. 2, pp. 182–195). Bandung: Masa Baru.

Whitehead, H. (1981). The Bow and the Burden Strap: A New Look at Institutionalized Homosexuality in Native North America. In S. Ortner & H. Whitehead (Eds.), *Sexual Meanings: The Cultural Construction of Gender and Sexuality* (pp. 80–115). Cambridge, UK: Cambridge University Press.

Wikan, U. (1990). *Managing Turbulent Hearts: A Balinese Formula for Living*. Chicago: University of Chicago Press.

Wilson, R. (2004). *I La Galigo* (Stage Play). Singapore.

Glossary

This glossary includes a list of the more frequently used foreign terms in this case study. The word is followed by an indication of language source: I for Indonesian; B for Bugis; E for English. Quite a few words now in common use in Indonesia derive from Arabic and Sanskrit, but I have signified them as Indonesian because they have been incorporated into the vernacular.

adat: I; custom, tradition, customary law.

adik: I; younger sibling.

agama: I; religion.

ajaib: I; miracle.

alat: I; tool, device, instrument.

ana' baccing: B; metal rhythm sticks.

anak buah: I; apprentice.

Andi: B; title signifying noble descent and high status, although lower status than *Puang*.

arajang: B; sacred regalia.

arisan: I; regular social gathering where members contribute money and take turns at winning the collective sum.

asli: I; real, original, authentic.

badi': B; small knife.

baju bodo: B; traditional blouse for women.

bakat: I; talent.

bangsawan: I; nobility.

Bapak: I; Father.

becak: I; pedicab.

bencong: I; slang word for transgender male.

béppa: B; cake.

berani: I; brave.

bissu: B; androgynous shaman.

bola monang: B; floating house.

bola riase': B; a house raised on pillars.

bonceng: I; to ride pillion.

Bu: I; Mrs.

Bugis: B; largest ethnic group in South Sulawesi.

bukan laki-laki: I; not men.

bule: I; foreigner.

Bupati: I; Regent or District Head.

cakep: I; handsome.

calabai: B; biological male who challenges masculine norms.

calalai: B; biological female who challenges feminine norms.

cenderung: I; inclined.

coli-coli: I; to masturbate.

dandan: I; grooming.

dangdut: I; a genre of Indonesian popular music partly derived from a mix of Arab, Indian, and Malay folk music.

darah putih: I; literally "white blood," representing noble lineage.

dewata: I; spirit, deity.

dimasuki: I; entered.

disurupi: I; entered by a spirit.

dukun beranak: I; midwife.

Haji: I; title indicating an individual who has made the pilgrimage to Mecca.

Hajj: I; the pilgrimage to Mecca.

hir: E; gender neutral form of his/her.

hunter: E; a term some calalai use to refer to themselves.

Ibu: I; Mother.

imam: I; religious leader or prayer leader.

Indo': B; Mother.

Indo' Botting: B; Wedding Mother (often calabai); managers of weddings and receptions.

jangan malu: I; "Don't be shy."

jilbab: I; Islamic head veil.

jiwa: I; soul, spirit.

kakak: I; elder sibling.

kancing: B; symbols.

kasar: I; rough, coarse.

kasih sayang: I; love and affection.

kebal: I; impenetrable.

kebaya: I; traditional Malay-style dress for women.

keberhalaan: I; idolatry.

kecenderungan: I; inclination.

kelamin: I; genitalia.

kepala ikan: I; fish head.

keris: I; wavy, double-bladed dagger.

kodrat: I; fate.

kos: I; a type of boarding house, often for students.

kuat: I; strong.

kue: I; cake.

lae-lae: B; bamboo rattle.

La Galigo: B; Bugis epic cycle that relates an envisaged past when spirits descended to the middle world to create order, similar in nature to Homer's *Iliad* or the *Ramayana*.

lamolong: B; altar.

lasogatta: B; rubber penis, dildo.

lawolo: B; thick, braided rope.

lesbi: E; lesbian.

lines: I; feminine partner of calalai.

loloni: B; dildo.

ma'giri': B; bissu test of spirit possession by self-stabbing.

magrib: I; evening Islamic prayers.

makkunrai: B; woman.

malebbi': B; noble, refined.

mampu: I; capable.

mangngelli dara: B; literally "to buy blood," meaning "to buy status."

manja: I; spoil, as in spoiling a child.

manusia: I; human.

Mas: I; title for a man, usually a relatively young man of equal or lesser status to the speaker.

mate siri': B; socially dead.

mesjid: I; mosque.

mujangka: B; medicine.

muncul: I; appear, emerge.

nasib: I; destiny.

nenek: I; grandparent, usually grandmother.

oroané: B; man.

pacaran: I; dating.

Pak: I; Mr.

pandai besi: I; blacksmith.

panggung: B; small temple.

passili: B; blessing.

pelacur: I; sex worker, prostitute.

pendamping: I; companion.

pētē-pētē: B; small minivan used for public transportation.

pria: I; man.

Puang: B; honorific title signifying very high status and noble descent.

Puang Lolo: B; assistant Puang Matoa.

Puang Matoa: B; highest rank bissu can attain.

punggawa: I; clerk.

roh: I; spirit, soul.

Rupiah (Rp): I; Indonesian currency; at the time of fieldwork US$1 = Rp10,000.

sahabat: I; close friend, partner.

sakit: I; ill, sick.

sakti: I; potent, powerful.

Sengkang: B; capital town of Wajo' district, South Sulawesi.

sesaji: I; ritual offerings.

s/he: E; gender-neutral form of she/he.

sifat: I; characteristic, nature, essential quality.

silsilah: I; genealogies.

simpanan: I; "a storage"; can imply "mistress."

siri': B; honor/shame complex.

sompa: B; payment made to a bride by the groom's family.

songkolo': B; sticky rice.

Sulawesi: B; island in Indonesia where I conducted fieldwork.

sunat: I; circumcision.

tau malisé: B; revered person.

tau massissi lalo: B; a person lacking desirable qualities; a low-status person.

to'ol to'olan: B; dildo.

tomboi: E; derived from the English and used by some calalai to refer to themselves.

tumba: B; a cylindrical drum.

Wajo': B; district or regency of which Sengkang is the capital.

wanita: I; woman.

wanita biasa: I; average or common woman.

wanita kasar: I; rough woman.

waria: I; derived from *wanita pria* (woman man); national term for transgender male.

Index